Write the

WINNING PROPOSAL

Patrick Dorsey

FACTUAL PLANET

SAINT LOUIS

ISBN 978-1-939437-56-3

Cover Illustration by Patrick Dorsey
Copyright © 2017 by Legendary Planet, LLC

Book design by Finscéal Welt
Typeset in Bell LT, Gill Sans MT, and Compacta

Manufactured in the United States of America

Factual Planet is an imprint of
Legendary Planet, LLC
PO Box 440081
Saint Louis, Missouri 63144-0081

LegendaryPlanet.com

Why the Big Margin?

Factual Planet books are designed to promote reader involvement and encourage the reader to get the most from the text.

To that end, all Factual Planet books employ an exceptionally wide margin on the outside edge of each page. Known in book design as a *scholar's margin*, it's useful for readers who want to make notes on a page as they read because it gives them the space to do so. (No more cramming thoughts around the author's name or the page numbers or showers of sticky notes falling out!)

So, please, take your favorite pen or pencil and make use of the space provided for your own notes, thoughts, and questions about the text presented.

Disclaimer

The advice contained in this material may not be suitable for everyone. The author designed the information to present his opinion and strategies on the subject matter. The reader must carefully investigate all aspects of any decisions before committing himself or herself or a business to any decision. The author obtained the information contained herein from sources he believes to be reliable, from his clients, and from his own professional and personal experience, but neither implies nor intends any guarantee of accuracy. The author is not in the business of giving legal, accounting, or any other type of professional advice. Should the reader need such advice, he or she must seek services from a competent professional. The author particularly disclaims any liability, loss, or risk taken by individuals or businesses who directly or indirectly act on the information herein. The author believes the advice presented here is sound, but readers cannot hold him or the publisher responsible for either the actions they take or the result of those actions.

Thanks to Ryan, Frank, Marla, Jacqui, Dionne, Jackie, Mike, Carrie, and everybody else I spent way too many hours with thrashing out and delivering winning proposals and responses. This book is here only because of what we all learned on deadlines at 1:30 in the morning...

Write the Winning Proposal

Contents

Chapter 1:
Why Pursue RFPs?

There is more potential today—probably more than ever before—to increase business and achieve success by responding to Requests For Proposals (RFPs).

As they have for decades now, both government agencies and private businesses rely increasingly on outsourcing to implement and complete projects. Whether it's a federal office looking for construction contractors to expand a facility, a state health department looking for managed care organizations to run their Medicaid operations, or a local tech company looking to put in place a new computer network, organizations are turning more and more to outside consultants and experts to get a job done.

And the way they find those experts? The RFP.

What's an RFP?

An RFP—sometimes called an RFQ (Request for Quote) or an ITN (Invitation to Negotiate) or any other acronym an issuer feels best describes what they're looking for— is a document an organization releases to invite bids from outside vendors or consultants for a product or service to solve a specified problem. Typically, the RFP describes a problem, need, or issue and includes detailed questions about how a respondent intends to handle or address the specifics of solving it. The RFP can be short and direct (one page with ten bullet points) or long and complicated (hundreds of pages of questions and sub-questions, with requests for thousands of pages of detailed supporting materials). RFPs usually have a set timeframe for the response and a strict due date, and sometimes very specific rules involving page layout, font size, and allowable word counts for responding proposals.

It sounds like a lot to deal with. And it can be, especially when working with government agencies that are required to issue RFPs and have concerns about transparency, appearance of impropriety, conflict of interest, and bureaucratic regulations that must be followed to the letter.

Want to get as close as you can to peeking at the other team's playbook? Read Michael Asner's book Bulletproof RFPs. *A guide for public entities that need to issue an RFP or similar document, it outlines the RFP process from writing and issuing to scoring and awarding business to successful respondents. For an RFP responder, it provides insight into the approach the people on the "other side" of the RFP take to invite solutions to the issues they face—and the better you understand an issuer's perspective, the better you can address their needs and persuade them to select you.*

But as a potential vendor, RFPs represent a doorway to contracts and opportunities. Literally billions of dollars in contract business are awarded every year through RFPs, representing not just new income but potential for new, ongoing business for your organization.

All you have to do to tap this opportunity and win the business is answer the issuer's questions with your proposal.

Your RFP Response— The Proposal

The key to winning business from an RFP is convincing the issuer that you're the best choice to do the work their RFP describes. And I hate to say this—so we might as well get it out of the way right now—but a great, well-priced solution often isn't enough to win the work. A great, well-priced, *and well-presented* solution, on the other hand...

That's where your RFP response—your proposal—comes in.

Allow me to break a communication rule for a moment and tell you what your proposal is *not*.

> *One of the first rules in writing effective messages: Use positive instructions.*
>
> *In other words, tell you audience what you want them to do. Negative instructions ("Don't do this," "Avoid that") emphasize the unwanted part of the message and put it at the forefront of the audience's thoughts. For example: if I told you "Don't think of the word rhinoceros for the next five minutes," what one word do you think would keep pushing its way to the center of your focus?*

Your proposal is not technical specs for your solution. It's not an outline of your customer programs. And it's not a recitation of client successes nor a pricing list.

It can, should—and most likely will—include all those things. But what it is...

...It's a *sales tool.*

Less a toothpaste ad and more a brochure for a new car (perhaps the lengthiest, most super-detailed brochure you ever picked up at the dealership, but a brochure nonetheless), you're kidding yourself if you say, "Our proposal has all the content and all the information that answers all their questions, so we're good!"

Information alone—even the exact information the issuer was hoping to see—isn't always enough to win that business.

Now, let's look at that car brochure.

You've probably read one before, so think through the impressions it left with you (and if you haven't, stop by a dealership and get one—heck, the salesperson will be thrilled to go through it with you, if you want).

Does the brochure just list the car's performance stats and pricing options? Or does it work, through slick images and careful arrangement of text in an attractive layout, to convince you *why* you that car is your *best* choice—that you need *that car* over any other?

Your proposal needs to convey a similar message.

Like any writing, some things are a matter of preference. But there are good and bad approaches—ways that work and ways that don't—to going about creating a proposal.

The chapters that follow walk you through methods—once you've qualified* an RFP and decided it's worth pursuing—to craft an irresistible document that will leave no doubt in a reviewer's mind that *you* are the best choice for the job.

---

* Qualifying an RFP—evaluating and choosing whether to pursue it—is a business decision that requires as much art as science on the part of the decision-makers. It includes knowledge of the issuer, of the problem to be addressed, and of the positions of any competitors. For example, the issuer may have already picked their winner and may be going through the motions of the RFP because of policy—you'll face an almost impossible effort selling yourself into such a situation. Not to mention when your solution isn't a good fit for the issuer's needs—no proposal, no matter how well put together, can win if, in the end, the solution is a bad fit. Researching and understanding these things lets you see whether an RFP is even worth spending time on, and helps you understand your organization's weaknesses and strengths in pursuing the business. Believe it or not, sometimes it makes better sense *not* to pursue certain business from certain potential clients. But qualifying is a whole other process, and something you need to work through completely before you start writing your winning proposal.

Chapter 2:
Assemble
Your Team

Like any task, to get the job done of completing
your winning RFP you need the right people.

There *are* business circumstances where the RFPs you're
writing proposals for are low-page-count, and you can
have one person answer questions and construct the
proposal, especially if that one person is dedicated to the
task, has few other responsibilities, knows your business
well, and is a solid writer.

In general, though—and for bigger RFPs in particular
—you need a team to write your proposal. And like any
good team, there are definite roles you need to fill in
order to take on a challenge and win.

Your Proposal Management Team is the group
dedicated to completing your response to the RFP you
want to win. Call them your Proposal Management
Team, Response Task Force, Business Development
Group, or RFP Gang, but note one word for certain in
that description: *dedicated*. If your team members are
always being pulled away to do other things, they
won't be able to focus on driving the proposal. From
when the RFP is released until its due date, the
individuals on this team need the approval and support
to make it their number-one priority.

Select Your Lineup

Who's on this team depends on your organization and goals, but typically a Proposal Management Team should include:

- **A manager**—someone with enough knowledge of your organization to identify needed resources and sources of information to answer questions and enough status within your business to get both the attention those resources when needed and cooperation from across the various levels of your organization. Whether specifically a project manager or simply a manager in charge of the proposal effort, this person is going to shepherd the project through your organization

- **A writer**—a professional and experienced writer who can organize all your information and details into clear, concise, understandable text. Skilled at interviewing experts and translating their thoughts for non-experts, a writer knows how to simplify and explain difficult concepts to a variety of readers and helps you find the holes in your explanations by identifying missing information that you know but a reader without your experience might not.

Sometimes, it's a hard sell getting a decision-maker to agree to hire a writer. When someone says, "We don't need a writer—everybody here has a college degree and knows how to write," remind that person that everybody there has completed Kindergarten, too, and knows how to use scissors—but you probably don't want any of them cutting your hair.

- **A member of executive management**—someone with executive knowledge of your organization's current business direction, to provide the team perspective and help qualify an RFP as to whether the potential business fits with your planned strategy.

- **Someone from Sales/Marketing**—not just to keep your marketing message and the proposal's message aligned, but also—more importantly—to help the team focus on the elements that are truly important to the issuer. This Sales/Marketing rep should be the one who's worked with the issuer directly and understands from conversations with the issuer's staff and decision-makers what the goals of the RFP are.

You'll need at least these four people on your team. Together, they can hash out everything that will drive both the big picture concerns and technical details of your proposal. Depending on your industry, you may also have others on the team such as an engineer, nurse, dental director, architect, software manager... basically, appropriate specialists from your organization to address those big picture concerns and technical details from an expert's perspective.

...Plus Your Secret Weapons

Remember how, at the beginning of every episode of *Mission: Impossible*, the team leader always sorts through files to select the agents needed for the assignment? Usually, it was always the same people—after all, every mission required electronics, disguise, and distraction—but, different missions sometimes called for different resources (MD virologist, archeologist, rocket propulsion engineer, opera soprano, whatever) and the team leader would rotate in an additional resource, someone the Impossible Mission Force would call on only when his or her particular set of skills was needed.

You need to do that for your Proposal Management Team, too.

Your Subject Matter Experts—SMEs for short—are those people you call on to help with specific response sections of the proposal. Though part of your organization, they aren't regular members of the Proposal Management Team. Rather, they're resources with specific knowledge of particular segments of your business who can give you detailed answers to certain questions in the RFP. Depending on your business, these resources could include:

- **An IT analyst who knows your data processing system exactly** and can diagram how your files move through your system and into the client's to update records.
- **An engineer who can explain how your solution can repair** the described damage, restore structural integrity, and prevent any further issues.
- **A Quality Assurance analyst who can describe completely** how your call center representatives are monitored and how their customer interactions are scored and fed back to them.
- **An IT manager who designed your data recovery plan** and can detail the steps your organization will follow to maintain service and shift services offsite in the event of a disaster.
- **An MD who can explain exactly the medical principles** underlying your proposed health program

and the reasons it's been successful for your other clients.

Again, your SMEs are anyone who has the information to answer a particular RFP question. Though not part of your regular team, they're every bit as important for when you need their specialized knowledge.

Now you have your team assembled. Time to get to work writing your proposal.

Chapter 3:
Three Steps to
Writing a Winning
Proposal

Really, there are only three steps to writing a winning proposal:

- ~~Preparation~~—Doing your homework to understand an RFP's questions, who you're writing to, and what you want to say about your solution's strengths
- **Writing**—Composing clear responses that answer the RFP questions compellingly
- **Editing**—Reviewing the response you wrote to ensure that it answers the RFP question completely and concisely and that it is written correctly

Of course, there are sub-steps to each of those three steps. (You didn't think all the other pages in this guide were for notes and flip-it doodles, did you?)

Preparation

Preparation involves three main tasks:

- Defining your Audience and your Message
- Reading the RFP and defining a Win Theme
- Breaking down the questions

Define Audience and Message

One thing is true for every writing project you will ever take on: Before you begin, you must define your Audience and your Message—in other words, ask yourself "Who am I talking to and what am I trying to tell them?"

Get out your highlighter and run it over those last thirteen words of that last sentence. Now draw stars around them, and if you're so inclined, little hearts as well.

That is the first Secret of Writing.

Got it? Good. Because, even beyond RFPs and proposals, it's a nugget of universal Writing Truth you need to carry with you for every writing project you ever take on. Whether it's a brochure or a cover letter or a PowerPoint show, and whether you're writing for advertising/marketing, technical/scientific, news/journalism, or grade school theatre, knowing your audience and your message to them—who you're talking to and what you're telling them—is vital and essential (and a whole lot of other redundant words I'm not going to run to my thesaurus to look up).

The word "talking" is used very specifically here. What you're doing in your response isn't sending the prospect information—you're engaging them in a conversation. We'll come back to this idea later, but still keep it in mind for now:

Audience

In answering the question *Who am I talking to?* you identify who's going to read and evaluate your proposal. Is it a manager? A corporate VP? An elected official?

A bureaucrat? A professional reviewer? Each of these audiences is different not just for who they are, but for what they're looking for in your proposal. And understanding what they're looking for will become key as you develop your overall theme for your proposal, which will ultimately shape all the answers.

In defining Audience, the research you did to qualify the RFP is the first place to start. For instance, whether the RFP is for a public or private sector project will be apparent from the RFP itself. Other information will take some thinking and some more active research, such as reviewing newspaper articles on elected or appointed officials leading the initiatives that resulted in the RFP being issued. Corporate reports and business journals can be a great source on company executives, as can press releases or newsletters from professional associations.

For example: for one Medicaid RFP I worked on as part of the Proposal Management Team, a quick bit of online research at the issuing state's website revealed that one of the lead players for the project wasn't just a politician, but also an MD. A little more research through his resume and a review of newspaper articles uncovered he was an MD who, before entering politics, had spent years working in the rural areas of his state to establish clinics and make medical care more accessible for the people living in those areas. This was important to the proposal because it told our team that, regardless of the statewide nature of the program and with no exceptional language regarding rural programs, one of the key decision-makers had a keen interest in the needs of rural populations. So to resonate with that leader, the proposal had best include very specific and concrete examples of how our proposed program would address and meet the needs of the people in the state's rural areas.

> *"What enables the enlightened...to achieve extraordinary success is foreknowledge."*
> *—Sun Tzu,* The Art of War

Another example: for an equipment proposal for a different project, our research began with the issuing organization's annual report and press releases. This uncovered the name and recent employment history of their newly-appointed COO. With her name and resume, further research through her previous employers' press releases and annual reports showed that she'd led efficiency and cost-cutting efforts for the last few companies she worked for. In this case, we could tell we had a decision-maker who was building her career on reducing costs and would be most interested in seeing the efficiencies and savings that would result from implementing our proposed solution.

Also, consider that different types of readers are looking for different information of different depths of detail. For an installation of a new network, the business-oriented CFO reviewing the proposal is most likely looking for different specifics than the VP of Information Technology—the first one is looking for numbers and information surrounding cost and ROI while the other is more concerned with capacity and throughput. Perhaps these are very broad generalizations, (today, the CFO in a tech company possibly holds a computer science degree, and the IT VP could be a former accountant whose interest in technology took her from one department to the other), but these examples should get you thinking about the type of information and the level of detail your proposal should convey and matching it to the readers who will be reviewing it.

Do your homework to get a better idea of who you're talking to before you decide on your message.

Message

Message is a little more straightforward than Audience. At the core, every RFP's Message is *We're the best to do this job for you.* But there's one little piece to add to the end of that, so the statement becomes *We're the best to do this job for you **because...***

It's after that *because...* that your work in defining your Message begins.

At this point, you need to work out what value—what *advantage*—you're offering the RFP's issuer. Beyond "because we really want your business!" what do you want the organization to whom you're writing this proposal to know about your solution? This point is tricky, because it's going to shape every answer in your proposal in some way.

> *Message isn't about you—it's about what the issuer wants and how you can help them solve the problem that led to the RFP. That also means it has to be unique for each proposal!*

Your best way to arrive at your message is to gather your leaders and coaches—your own organization's managers, sales and marketing reps, and subject matter experts—and hammer out your Message for this prospect together. I'd recommend a conference room, a white board, box lunches, and a locked door, but that's only because I've seen how easy it is to distract an organization's important, key players from this task—which in the end will be central to every answer you write. Defining your Message is an important step, so get the commitment from your participants, take the time to think it through, and do it.

Your Message is a brief summary of the strong points of your organization's solution. What is it that sets you apart from the competition? Don't answer that question like an engineer and turn in a well-thought-out list of bullet points (though that's a good way to start thinking it through). Answer it like a romance novel writer: what feeling do you want the reviewer to have about your proposal? Are you

- The least expensive?
- The most experienced?
- The biggest player?
- The one with the best-developed program?
- The most attentive to customers?
- The most hands-on in a field of outsourcers?
- The only local vendor?
- The scrappy up-and-comer in a field of bloated establishment players?
- The only one big enough for the job?

Think of your message as the back cover description of a book. Or better yet, the Netflix description of a movie—just a sentence or two that can be read in under ten seconds to get across what you want your reviewer to know. For example,

- **If your strength is lower cost:** "Our use of technology creates economies of scale that result in cost savings."
- **If your strength is innovation:** "We offer innovative programs no one else has that both lower costs and increase results."
- **If your strength is you're already a long-term partner who's re-bidding**: "We've been a faithful partner with the state's health plan for over 15 years, since inception of the program."

You want to keep it brief and direct, but don't worry about being clever and pithy. This is a summary for your team to use internally to define what you want to tell the reviewers. Working out your Message and writing it down gets everyone who's answering the RFP on the same page about what your organization's strengths are as you wade into the proposal. It's also a good first step toward developing your Win Theme.

Read the RFP

You're saying to yourself "Duh! *Of course* I'm going to read the RFP!"

Hang with me…

When you say you're going to read it, do you mean the sections assigned to you to answer, or the entire RFP? If you're on the Proposal Management Team, you need to read the whole RFP, from cover to cover.

Yes, it's a lot more reading. Yes, it's stuff that you personally aren't answering and has nothing to do with your area of expertise. *"I'm the finance director—"* I hear you crying out now, *"—why do I need to read all the stuff in the IT section about file transfers? I don't even know what CSV and delimited mean, let alone the difference* between them!"*

It's extra work, and some of it may be unintelligible to you. But it will pay off because two things happen when

---

* Delimited flat files have a delimiter character separating the values; CSV files do, too, but add an enclosing character before and after each value. Just FYI if you were interested, since I brought it up.

you read the entire RFP:

- You see the "big picture" of what the RFP is asking for
- You get another set of eyes on it

The Big Picture

"But I'm just answering these three questions," you're saying, "I don't need to read the whole RFP."

To *just* answer the questions, yes, you're right.

To answer the questions *correctly*—in the full context of what the RFP issuer is looking for—you need to read the entire RFP.

Why?

Because any one question—or two or three—may not reflect the full intent of the RFP. Like any lengthy, complicated written document—from a billionaire's pre-nup to Joyce's *Ulysses*—you have to read between the lines. You have to look beyond the plain, superficial meaning of the text for the intent behind it. Remember in high school English, when you read books and short stories to identify theme, imagery, symbolism, foreshadowing, and all that literary stuff? Believe it or not, there's some of that in almost every written document, even an RFP.

Read the RFP. Look for things that are repeated and keep note of them. An RFP that consistently mentions savings, reduced expenses, and other similar concerns throughout is doing it for a reason. Even if being the low-cost or most cost-saving solution isn't stated, it's clearly of importance to the questions' writers, and probably the issuer. Similarly, if the RFP keeps mentioning quality of service (or some variation) or low complaint/low maintenance, keep track of it.

Note the things you see repeated like this and talk them over with your Proposal Management Team to see how you can reflect and address these underlying, unstated requirements in your answers.

A complete read of the RFP can also point you to areas to address that you may not have thought of. Perhaps a question not assigned to you prompts you to consider a tangent point in one of the questions that is assigned to you. For example, reading a question on file back-ups might prompt you to consider additional content in a question that you're answering on disaster recovery.

Read All the Attachments, Exhibits, and Appendices

When I said the whole thing, I wasn't kidding. Information is going to be scattered all through the RFP.

For example, there might be a table in an appendix of the RFP that lists all the specific file transfer protocols the issuer is requiring in any proposed new network implementation, along with their minimum acceptable file transfer speeds.

Never assume someone else spotted something you spotted, and never be afraid to point it out. On the flipside, never take any feedback personally. You're part of a team and you're all working together to make the best, most complete response to the RFP and win business.

If Question 46 asks you to outline the proposed system's data transfer protocols but doesn't mention the required protocols and speeds by name or refers you to the appendix for them, there's a chance—a good chance—your answer may not include all the information they want to see. Because of that, your response doesn't answer the question completely and you won't get full points when it's scored.

Believe me, a few points here and there add up. They can make the difference between you and one of your competitors getting the contract. It's one thing to lose an opportunity because your proposed solution wasn't as good a match as the other guy's. But when you lose because you consistently missed points for leaving pieces out of your answers...as I tell my SMEs on any project, we want to leave no points on our desks and answer every question as completely as we can. So read everything.

More Eyes on the Document to See More

Here's another Secret of Writing most writers will confirm: The more eyes you can get on a document, the better.

Usually, this refers to editing. But it's also exceptionally helpful when reviewing an RFP. We all read and process information differently. We all bring our own pre-conceptions to what we read, and we all get distracted at different points when reading. So, the more people you can have review a document, the better your chance that nothing gets overlooked.

This is important because those additional sets of eyes may help you uncover something, an angle or element, everyone else missed. It takes only one person to see it and call attention to it for the rest of the group. Remember, RFPs are often written by a team unaccustomed to writing such a document or by a hired consultant who knows RFP writing but maybe not the issuer's industry or niche. In the first situation, something may not stand out as much as needed due to lack of writing skill and experience; in the second, it may be underemphasized for lack of understanding of its importance. Either way, it's not standing out the way readers may expect it to, so it's easy to overlook.

I remember reading one RFP when I was still new with an organization and being struck by a phrase buried toward the bottom of a paragraph that sounded to me like it was saying that not meeting a certain goal would require us (the submitters) to pay cash penalties. I highlighted it on my copy and brought it up at our next Proposal Management Team meeting.

"Well, no, that's not what they're requiring there," one VP said, squinting again at the RFP.

"I dunno," said the director at the other side of the table. "It kinda might..."

"Let me read it again," said our teleconferenced representative from the Legal Department.

We ended up submitting a clarifying question to the issuer. But the potential penalty clause got past two VPs, a director, a lawyer, and a few others. And to be honest, the only reason I caught it was because I was way less familiar with the industry and its lingo and what they had all taken one way, I had taken another. For sure, it was something worth asking.

> It varies from one to the next, but most RFPs have a process for respondents to ask questions to clarify uncertain points in the RFP. Unless stated otherwise, you're better off gathering your questions together and submitting a list of several questions, rather than dribbling them in one after the other, one at a time, so the issuer grows tired of seeing your name pop up and then starts to dread it.

Schedule a Kickoff Meeting and Table Reading

I'm not one for holding any more meetings than absolutely necessary, believe me. But sometimes, getting all your team, plus any additional players, all in the same room at the same time is the best way to get everybody on the same page (or at least in the same proposal). At this meeting, together you all do what I call a "table reading."

Begin by sending a copy of the RFP along with the meeting invitation to all the members of your Proposal Management Team so everyone has a chance to read it ahead of time (or at least the SMEs read their assigned sections). Make sure you schedule a few hours for this meeting because you're all going to read through the entire RFP together.

Time-consuming, yes. But it gets everyone talking about their individual observations and concerns about the RFP, which ultimately helps everyone see the various sections through the eyes of the person assigned to it. Perhaps this isn't terribly realistic for a small proposal, but even if it's just you and your SME, try to get this time together.

A quick exercise to use while you have all your players gathered: Go around the room and ask each person to state your solution's greatest strength. Write down each person's response, then go around the room again and get each person's idea of the RFP issuer's main problem or pain—the reason they've issued the RFP. Comparing those lists, you can identify how your strengths align with solving their problem.

The more your team communicates, whether two people or twenty, the better all the responses are and the more all involved feel—and act—like a team. Don't underestimate team spirit. You'd be surprised how differently resources treat the proposal writer who's pestering them for answers vs. a teammate they're working with to win business.

Define a Win Theme for Your Proposal

Now that you've all read the RFP and have discerned what the issuer is asking for, you can distill the Message you established into a Win Theme for your proposal. Previously, we defined the Message as the Netflix description of your proposed solution. The Win Theme, then, is your tag line.

> *What's a tag line? In marketing and advertising, it's a brief, memorable phrase about your solution that's easy for your audience to remember.*

Staying with our movie analogy, tag lines are concise and striking for the image or emotion they immediately evoke. For examples, here are some taglines that were used as part of the advertising for a few well-known movies:

- "One man's struggle to take it easy."
  Ferris Bueller's Day Off (1986)
- "There are 3.7 trillion fish in the ocean. They're looking for one."
  Finding Nemo (2003)
- "The last man on Earth is not alone."
  I Am Legend (2007)

An effective tag line, as you can see, is only a few words yet still impactful and descriptive.

Your Win Theme will become your proposal's tagline. More than a distillation of your message, your Win Theme is a quick, evocative description of the advantage of your solution, said in just several words. It states not only what your strength is, but wraps the statement in a context that sets it immediately and memorably into your reader's mind. Appearing throughout your proposal, it will shape the reader's impression of your solution. It will be part of your cover letter and executive summary. It will be displayed on your cover and in either the header or footer of every page of the proposal. It will shade almost every answer you compose.

So it's important that you get it right.

Like the Message, the Win Theme should be developed and determined by the leaders and coaches on the response team, working together as a group. The Win Theme is tied so very closely to your Message that you might be tempted to develop them together, but you should wait. Each step so far has helped you define understanding. With Audience and Message, you decided who you're talking to and what you want to tell them. In reading the RFP, you looked at your audience and discerned what it is they're looking for from you. Now with the Win Theme, you're deciding how to make your message resonate with that audience so they view you as the obvious, best choice.

The Win Theme is short, focused, impactful, and immediately clear. Let's go back to our sample Message statements and craft a Win Theme for each:

- **Message:** "Our use of technology creates economies of scale that result in cost savings."

  ▶ **Win Theme:** "Technical Solutions to Improve Your Bottom Line"

- **Message:** "We're high-touch and our service is always person-to-person for the best customer experience."

  ▶ **Win Theme:** "In-Person Support Tailored for You"

- **Message:** "We've been a faithful partner with the state's health plan for over 15 years, since inception of the program."

  ▶ **Win Theme:** "15 Years of Service and Caring"

What makes you the one fish among trillions or the last man on Earth who finds he's not alone? Think about what your potential client *really wants* from this RFP (which you already know from developing your Message) and how you can tell it in under ten words.

> *Winning Public Sector Win Themes are usually personal—centered on the public as people, focused on care or service, and highlighting long-term relationships with the state agency.*

The Win Theme shapes everything you write in your proposal. As you state your case to the reader, it defines the reasons to cite and the kind of proof to incorporate— examples, data, and anecdotes—in order to guide the reviewers to see why your solution is best and compel them to select you. Be sure to spend the time you need to develop your Win Theme.

> *Think of your Audience when you develop your Win Theme—an RFP for a military communications contract requires a different feel than one for a state healthcare contract!*

Break Down the Questions

Back to the RFP.

At this point, you now understand and have defined:

- Who you're talking to (Audience)
- What you want them to know about you (Message)
- What their underlying need is (from reading the RFP front-to-back)
- How to tell them you can address that need (Win Theme)

Now, it's time to start answering their questions. This process begins by assigning questions to each member of the Proposal Management Team, including your SMEs. Each person then reviews his or her assigned questions and breaks each one down.

So we're on the same page, let's discuss what "breaking down" a question means when we're talking about answering an RFP.

Read the Question and Look for Clues

You've read the entire RFP and have a sense of what the underlying need is. Now, read the questions assigned to you. Make mental or written notes, or highlight it as you read.

The first thing you're looking for in the question is the overall gist of it. Sum up for yourself what you think they're asking for with the question. Do this so you can be sure you're addressing their needs, not your selling points.

Note Their Language

Note the language the question uses. You want to be sure to use their words and terminology in your responses to their questions.

For example, our proposal team for one project had a contact who insisted that the word "partner" (as in "We plan to partner with you to create success…") was strictly a legal term that implied a contractual relationship (agree with him or not, he isn't the only one I've heard take that stance). So for issuers who hold the same opinion, note whether the language says "We would like to partner with a vendor…" vs. "We would like to team with a vendor…" and use their same language in your response. This is true with words like *stock* vs. *inventory, product* vs. *merchandise, client* vs. *customer, data* vs. *file,* and many, many others. Repeating their phrasing and using their terminology help promote a connection between you and the reviewer through the *Echo Effect*.

Use the Echo Effect to Build Connection with the Reviewer

The Echo Effect is a psychological principle that demonstrates how repetition of words in an interaction increases people's positive feelings and behaviors toward those mirroring their words. Taking advantage of the Echo Effect, you always want to repeat the issuer's choice of words in your response to help create in the reviewers' minds (consciously or unconsciously) a sense of your organization being in sync with theirs—they'll feel that you understand and care about the same issues they do. The Echo Effect has also been demonstrated to increase a listener's sense of liking someone and wanting to work with that person, with one study even showing that waitresses who make effective use of echoing earn larger tips!

Making your point using the RFP language can help the reviewer feel that you "get" them, that you're in sync with how they view and do things. Again, this is all unconscious, but when reviewers finish reading your answer, you want them to have the impression you understand their need for a partner vs. a teammate (whichever word they used in the RFP) better than a competing proposal that opted to use the word the issuer didn't choose—and may be less comfortable with.

It sounds a little contrary to concern yourself with feelings and impressions in a fact-filled document, but remember, your RFP response is a sales tool, and any sales rep will tell you that closing a sale is based on the buyer's feelings.

Learn your prospect's vocabulary and use their words to help them feel more positively about your proposed solution to their problem.

Create a List of Question Points to Address

Most questions in the RFP are laid out simply as a paragraph instructing respondents on various considerations to include in the answer. Read through the paragraph, and list each item you think it's asking for.

If you're lucky, the question is laid out as a numbered or bulleted list. If that's the case, take each numbered or bulleted item as a question detail to answer.

When you're finished, for each question you'll have a list of specific items to address in your answer.

Select a Style Guide

Do this up front. You'll be happy later.

A style guide's main purpose is to create consistency in how your materials present information. It defines all the rules for how your document should look and read, such as the fonts to use, spelling and capitalization, page layout and spacing, what colors to use and when, placement of graphics, and even specific words or phrases to use or avoid.

Professional Consistency

Ensuring consistency is important in customer-facing materials because consistency creates an impression of professionalism. If the font changes from one paragraph to the next, if your headings are blue on some pages and black on others, if diagrams are centered on the page in some places and flushed left on other pages, your proposal communicates to the reader that you're sloppy and disorganized.

Do you think anyone wants to give business to a disorganized partner with sloppy work?

But Who Cares About Consistency?

"I've never noticed fonts or what text is colored which way," some of you are saying, "so, really how many people reading the proposal do?"

Among reviewers, more of them notice than you think. But even if your readers are like you and don't think they notice, they actually do, even without realizing

Consistency does two things for your proposal: it creates a "single voice" for the reviewer reading it, and it makes it easier for the reviewer to process and understand the information you're working to get across.

By "one voice" what I mean is this: suppose you're attending a slide show presentation. After every slide or two, the presenter turns the presentation over to a different presenter, each one with slides laid out differently than the others'—one has plain white slides with bold black text and each point bulleted out while another uses a mountain graphic as the background on her slides, with a big block of white text set in the middle of every page, while another presenter has a white background but uses, red, blue, and yellow text, with each color signifying the sub-level of the text, and then there's yet another presenter with a different style, and then back to the second presenter…and none, you realize, use the same terms for the product they're presenting on…

You can see how that would be a little jarring, with each presenter telling a different part of the story in a different way. But it's how a reader perceives your proposal if you don't have consistent formatting and consistent writing.

Consistency also helps your reader understand you better. Besides cutting down the confusion of different voices explaining things, when your pages are consistent readers can develop a sense of what you're doing to present information and learn your document's rules for how everything is organized. If those rules change every few pages and sometimes change back, it means every time things change, the reader has to re-process the rules. This isn't a conscious thing (unless your various sections are *wildly* different) but it does slow the reader down and make your proposal feel harder to read.

You need a style guide.

Find a Style Guide

If you're part of a large organization (or a smaller one that's on top of things) there's probably already a style guide in place. All you need to do is ask where to find a copy.

If for some reason your organization doesn't have a style guide, you can create your own. All you need to do is design your basic page and document all the rules around it, so whoever is writing, revising, or laying out your proposal content can find your standards and consult them when needed.

Some of you just took a breath and stopped when you were reading those last couple lines. Relax, and exhale. Even if you never heard the term *style guide* until you got to that last paragraph, it's easy to put one in place—you can buy one. Anywhere you can buy or at least order books, you can purchase style guides such as *The Chicago Manual of Style*, *The AMA Style Guide*, or *The Gregg Reference Manual*. Use one of those (or any one you prefer) as the basis for your style guide. Then just define a few rules specific to what you want for your proposals ("First-level headings are 16 point Calibri bold and second-level headings are 14 point Calibri italic," "Center all charts and diagrams.") and declare "For all other matters, see *The AMA Style Guide* (or whichever guide you selected).

Ready to Write!

So now you have an understanding of the RFP with its overarching goal and underlying needs. You've defined how your solution meets the RFP's goal and needs, and you've broken down the questions so you know all the specific points the RFP is asking you to address.

Time to get writing!

Writing

Writing is where the serious work of your proposal begins (the title of this book isn't *Research the Winning Proposal* or *Discuss the Winning Proposal*—the first word is *Write* is for a reason). Writing is where you're going to take everything you've reviewed and met over and decided on and really craft the answers that are going to convince the issuer or their reviewers that you are the most capable of helping them solve their problems and meet their goals.

Start Your Answer With Their Question

Copy the question from the RFP and put it right at the start of your answer. Every time.

The most import reason to do this is the only one that matters: It reminds the reader of *exactly* which question you're answering while providing a quick reference for the reader on the specifics of the question.

Also, if you put the question in bold or in a box or in color (whatever fits the layout you've designed), it then becomes essentially a heading in your proposal. Your readers can then use it to find their place in your document, either when looking for a particular question to score or for when they're reading a response and want to check your answer against a related question.

Psychologically, again, this also lets you employ the Echo Effect to build up the reader's feeling of connection with you.

Create an Outline for Your Response

Start writing the way your third grade teacher taught you—with an outline. Outlining your answer first helps you organize all the specific details you want to cover in your answer and helps you make sure you don't leave anything out. The good thing right now is you've already started your outline. Remember when you broke down each question into the individual points it's asking for?

That was also the first step in creating your outline for each question.

Keep Your Answers in the Order Asked

The outline helps ensure your response includes *all* the bits of information the question is asking for *in the order they were asked*. Picture the reviewers reading through your proposal and scoring it with a checklist—you want to make it easy for them to find each item on their checklist in your answer and mark it off without hunting around.

That's not just metaphor. Frequently, that's *exactly* how a reviewer reads the responses. Whether scoring an electronic file on screen or a printed copy in a big, three-inch loose leaf binder, reviewers usually have a sheet at hand to score each answer as they read—a score sheet that's typically prepared by breaking down the questions and putting a box next to each item for a checkmark, grade, or point value.

Write Your Answer

With the question broken down and your answer outlined it's time to get down to writing.

If you're a writer, this is what you do, so get to it.

If you're not, relax. Take a deep breath, and exhale. This is a proposal, not an entry for the Pulitzer—nobody is looking for sparkling prose, wit, or insight. They just want an explanation of how your solution will solve their problem.

Remember I mentioned before that you're engaging the reader in a conversation? Just do that. Think of how you'd talk it through with someone at your desk. You already have it outlined, so you know all things you want to say and in what order you need to say them. Now write it.

Never use canned answers!

Sometimes, when you realize you've answered a certain question in a previous RFP response, you'll be tempted to grab that old answer and drop it into the current proposal.

Don't.

Yes, there are programs out there that let you create a giant warehouse of old answers you can search and re-use. But if your answer doesn't align with the question, it won't feel right to a reviewer and will cost you points.

You can certainly use information from old proposal answers, but always re-write them to the current RFP questions in front of you!

Use Their Words

Always mirror a question's language in you answer. Aside from the advantages in creating a sense of connection with the reader through the Echo Effect (as we discussed in "Use the Echo Effect to Build Connection with the

Reviewer"), using the same words as the question also makes it easier for the reader to locate the key points in your answer—they're the words the reader already has in mind.

Readers also more readily understand what you say when you use the words they're expecting—change their words in your answer, and they have to spend time and cognitive energy mapping the words you substituted to the ones used in the question.

Some of you are doubting this. "Seriously, how long can it take to mentally substitute *partner* for *team up*—how much extra work is it really?" you ask. But trust me, it's about the overall impression, unconscious or pre-conscious, that your answer is leaving with the reviewer. Any time you make a reviewer think or take time to make connections between your words and theirs, they're not taking in your message of "Our solution is the best because..." and you've wasted an opportunity to convince that reviewer.

Use their words to help them navigate and understand your responses.

Guide the Reader with Subheadings

If your response to a certain part of the question is buried in a big paragraph, the reviewer might not see it. Call attention to each element in your answer using subheadings. Like street signs, subheadings help readers find their way to the specific information they're looking for.

The following pictures oversimplify a bit, but they make the point: which layout makes it easier to find Item A,

Item B, and Item C on the page? With subheadings, it's apparent at a glance:

Item A Lorem ipsum dolor sit amet, consectetur adipiscing elit, sed do eiusmod tempor incididunt ut labore et dolore magna aliqua. Ut enim ad minim veniam, quis nostrud exercitation ullamco laboris nisi ut aliquip ex ea commodo consequat. Item B Duis aute irure dolor in reprehenderit in voluptate velit esse cillum dolore eu fugiat nulla pariatur. Excepteur sint occaecat cupidatat non proident, sunt in culpa qui officia Item C deserunt mollit anim id est laborum.Lorem ipsum dolor sit amet, consectetur adipiscing elit, sed do eiusmod tempor incididunt ut labore et dolore magna aliqua. Ut enim ad minim Item C veniam, quis nostrud exercitation ullamco laboris nisi ut aliquip ex ea commodo consequat.

Item A
Lorem ipsum dolor sit amet, consectetur adipiscing elit, sed do eiusmod tempor incididunt ut labore et dolore magna aliqua. Ut enim ad minim veniam, quis nostrud exercitation ullamco laboris nisi ut aliquip ex ea commodo consequat.

Item B
Duis aute irure dolor in reprehenderit in voluptate velitesse cillum dolore eu fugiat nulla pariatur. Excepteur sint occaecat cupidatat non proident, sunt in culpa qui officia

Item C
Deserunt mollit anim id est laborum.Lorem ipsum dolor sit amet, consectetur adipiscing elit, sed do eiusmod tempor incididunt ut labore et dolore magna aliqua.Ut enim ad minim

Keep to Your Outline

As you write, you may be tempted to start moving things around. "This idea here would make more sense with that one over there," you might think. Or, "Those two points can be combined into one."

Stop, and back away from the keyboard.

If the question asks for A, B, C, and D, your answer should proceed from A to B to C to D. You outlined the answer in that order for a reason—it's the order in which the information was asked, and more importantly, it's the order in which the reviewer is looking for each part.

Remember that checklist they're probably using to score your answer?

If the reviewer doesn't see an answer where he or she expects it because you combined it with another item later in the response, he or she marks a zero on the scoresheet.

When it turns up later, where you combined it with the other item, will that reviewer go back up the list and put the points in, replacing the initial zero? Probably. Will the reviewer feel annoyed, even unconsciously, and give you fewer points for making him or her stop, go back to find the line to re-score, and revise it? Possibly. And that's assuming the reviewer even connects the information in the combined response with the "missing" response he or she didn't see before. So you may still get the zero.

Your job is to make sure the reviewer has an easy time finding everything in your answer. If the RFP asks for A, B, C, and D, give them A, B, C, and D, in that order and clearly labelled.

Break Up Large Pages of Text

Long, text-heavy paragraphs are nearly never the most effective way to get information across to your reader. Think about a college text book you open to find densely worded pages of explanation, with long sentences filling each page from top to bottom and margin to margin.

In school, you read books written that way because you had to. And they were written that way because the authors and editors knew you had to read them, so they didn't put in the work to make the text accessible.

But you're writing a proposal—a sales document, remember?—and your reader doesn't *have* to read it, nor is it the reader's job to discern the important points and subtleties of your writing. So if you lose readers at any point, it's not their problem. It's yours.

On top of that, text-heavy pages can be intimidating to a reader "What kind of slog will this be?" or "How am I going to get through all this before I have to get home and let the dog out?" may be the questions your readers ask quietly as they turn the page. If they're worried about getting through the document, they're not focusing on your content. Or feeling very positive about you and your solution.

You need to keep them engaged, and focused on how well your solution solves their issue, not on how much longer they're going to have to read your answer.

The subheads discussed above will help. Breaking up the text, they transform one long, long page into a few focused paragraphs. The more you can cut your information into bite-sized pieces, the less time and effort the readers have to devote to cutting it up themselves and the more they can focus on your content. This way, you're doing more than giving them information—you're helping them process it.

Consider the Best Way to Answer the Question

The goal of your proposal is not to write answers but to present information effectively and convincingly, so always look for better ways to show it on a page. Bulleted lists, numbered steps, and graphics are all highly effective ways to present information so readers can take it in quickly. Plus, changing things up using these methods not only keeps the reader engaged, but can also show your information in ways helpful to readers with different learning styles.

There are four kinds of learners according to the VARK education model: Visual, Auditory, Reading/ Writing, and Kinesthetic. Each type of learner takes in information best in one of those learning styles. Yes, it's a written proposal, but look for alternate ways to engage your reader's attention, with graphics—or if it's an electronic document, links to video or audio content such as animation showing how your mobile device conveys data to your collector for processing or a song for your children's fitness program to encourage kids to dance.

Bulleted Lists

When you have an answer that lists a number of points throughout a long paragraph, consider making it into a bulleted list. A bulleted list not only breaks up the visual monotony of answers that go on for line after line, paragraph after paragraph, it also makes it easier for readers to pick out a specific item they're looking for. For example, in which list below can you scan and locate individual items more quickly?

Our Fruit Offerings

Seasonally, our fruit choices include apples, pears, oranges, cherries, persimmons, bananas, melon, peaches, strawberries, and blueberries.

Item B

Duis aute irure dolor in reprehenderit in voluptate velitesse cillum dolore eu fugiat nulla pariatur. Excepteur sint occaecat cupidatat non proident, sunt in culpa qui officia

Item C

Deserunt mollit anim id est laborum. Lorem ipsum dolor sit amet, consectetur adipiscing elit, sed do eiusmod tempor incididunt ut labore et dolore magna aliqua. Ut enim ad minim

Our Fruit Offerings

Seasonally, our fruit choices include:

- apples
- pears
- oranges
- cherries
- persimmons
- bananas
- melons
- peaches
- strawberries
- blueberries

Item B

Duis aute irure dolor in reprehenderit in voluptate velitesse cillum dolore eu fugiat nulla pariatur. Excepteur sint occaecat cupidatat non proident, sunt in culpa qui officia

Item C

Deserunt mollit anim id est laborum. Lorem ipsum dolor sit amet, consectetur adipiscing elit, sed do eiusmod tempor

Numbered Lists

Similar to a bulleted list, a numbered list breaks up paragraphs to add interest to a page while making it easier for a reader to find each item listed. Although some people use the two lists interchangeably, I use numbered lists only when I want to indicate the items in the list *need* to be in the numbered order shown, whether prioritizing them (where the first item is the most important in the list) or because they're steps that have to be taken in that particular order to accomplish a task.

Graphics

Remember that highlighter I had you get out back when we were discussing Audience and Message? Get it out again and highlight the next sentence:

Unless the RFP specifically forbids them, your proposal *must* have graphics, and you should use them whenever possible.

Yes, I have seen RFPs that said, "The submitter should refrain from pictures or illustrations of any kind in their response." But those are only slightly less frequent than Bigfoot sightings and should be treated as exceptions, not SOP, for your proposals.

Any time you can illustrate your point, do it! According to the Visual Teaching Alliance, the brain processes visual information in a fraction of the time it takes to read and process text, and visual information is more easily remembered. So any time you use a visual, your readers take in the information faster and retain it better.

By breaking up the text with a picture of some kind, you re-engage your readers and relieve their fatigue from reading pages and pages of text. You also get the opportunity to more strongly involve those readers who process information better visually than by reading.

By graphics, I mean any image that isn't paragraph text. This can include:

- **Charts and diagrams**—Line graphs, bar graphs, pie charts, scattergrams, flow charts, organization charts, and maps all express information visually, and typically, in less space than the text you'd use to say the same thing. With the right illustration, the cliché about a picture being worth a thousand words is completely true. So if you ever have to choose between using paragraph and a chart, go with the chart.
- **Photos**—Research shows human brains are hardwired to respond to faces, and that smiling faces stimulate a reward reaction in the brain. Want your reviewer to feel good reading your proposal? Use smiling faces on the cover and throughout. If the RFP asks for resumes or even just quick bios of key players, include a smiling shot of each person as part of the layout. And if you can include photos of your customers smiling (at an event, during a service call, etc.)…well, now you've not only made your readers feel good, but also left them with the impression your customers are happy. Think about that car brochure again—does anyone in the pictures ever look less than delighted, whether it's a new convertible or a minivan?
- **Art**—Logos from your product partners or accrediting organizations can catch a reader's eye and convey associations instantly, while screenshots from your website or pages from your handbook can show exactly how above-the-rest your customer-facing materials

are. Got a mascot? A drawing of it can help lock-in your organization in the reader's memory.

- **Callouts**—Situated so they stand out from the other text on the page, callouts alert your reader to a specific point or highlight an important idea so it stands out from the rest of the page.

Even though they're made up of text, by using a box or other graphical element combined with a different typeface than the body of the proposal—in color if possible—a callout can break up long stretches of paragraph text the same way a graphic does.

Where do you get graphics? Most reporting tools these days export pie charts and bar graphs and other standard charts. For things like logos or photos, check with your marketing group. For other illustrations, you can purchase stock photos and art from various sites online, but custom art may require you to commission an artist.

Be Specific and Back Up What You Claim

Anybody can say "buy our product" or "engage our services." Most will think to tack on "because we're an industry leader" or "for outstanding quality." Everything from ketchup to automobiles to hand lotion makes such grand assurances of excellence and superiority. But do you take ads that promise "the best" or "highest quality" or "finest" or "life-changing" at their word?

Of course you don't. You do as we here in Missouri do, and you say, "Show me."

The people reading your proposal say the same thing. And not just the reviewers. I was working on a proposal recently for a client and the project's lead consultant was reviewing the SMEs' responses with me when he looked up, peeled off his reading glasses tiredly, and sighed, "They're just making unsubstantiated statements."

This was their project consultant. The guy on their side, trying to help them win the business, and even *he* got to the Show-me Point with their answers.

The good news is, the solution to listing superlatives is simple. The bad news is, it's more work: After every declaration you make about "best-in-class" or "industry leadership," after every claim to the top spot, or any use of the words "unparalleled" or "unmatched"—

—explain *why*.

If you really are the best or the top, that's easy to substantiate with scores and awards. If your tools and methods really are unique, you can refer to your patents or copyrights that make them proprietary. If you can't back it up…why, again, should your reader believe you?

Describe the Successes You Create for Your Clients

Here's another secret to keep in mind as you write your answer: your clients and prospects don't really care how well you do *anything*. They don't care how fast your turnaround times are, and they don't care how high industry journals rank you, or how much your member satisfaction outpaces the competition.

What they want to know is the *advantage* of selecting you—that is to say, how you'll solve their problem. Instead of telling a reader how successful you are, talk about how clients benefit from how well you do things.

What's the difference?

- **Not:** "Our data recovery service is unmatched."

    ▶ **Instead:** "None of our clients has ever lost data after signing up with us."

- **Not:** "We have the fastest turnaround time in the industry."

    ▶ **Instead:** "Our industry-leading turnaround time reduces our clients' waiting time and related expenses."

- **Not:** "We have the highest member satisfaction scores in the state."

    ▶ **Instead:** "We have the highest member satisfaction scores in the state, exceeding mandated goals for any state nationwide."

Use the "Pain Island" model to think through what your customers want from you. As described by Vrinda Normand, in this model, your customers are all on Pain Island, a terrible place they want to escape, and you have a boat you can sell them seats on. What you need to understand is those customers don't want to buy a boat or go for a boat ride—they want to get off Pain Island. All your descriptions of your boat, then, should tell them how your boat is best for getting them off Pain Island. They don't care about the fine leather seats on your boat, but whether there are enough comfortable, pain-free seats for them. They don't care about the horsepower of the engine, but how fast and reliably it can get them away from Pain Island. Figure out what your customers' Pain Island is, and then explain your features in a way that shows how they help your customers get away from it.

Even Better: *Back It Up with Numbers*

We've taken the vague claims and turned them into features that show your prospects immediately how they'll benefit from working with you. If you really want to impress them, back that up now with numbers.

In evaluation, data is king. Something that's just a load of superlatives tells reviewers nothing—what they're looking for is a solution from someone with a history of success. The vendor who can use numbers to make a point has the advantage—experience and stability usually* beat flash and "awesomeness," so give them the numbers that demonstrate your successes, and the sources for them, too.

- **Good:** "None of our clients has ever lost data after signing up with us."
  - ▶ **Better:** "Out of the 5,000 clients we've served in the last 10 years, not one has lost data."
- **Good:** "Our industry-leading turnaround times reduce our clients' waiting time and related expenses."
  - ▶ **Better:** "Our average turnaround time is 2.5 days (less than half the industry-typical 6 days), reducing the expenses associated with waiting by 30%."
- **Good:** "We have the highest member satisfaction scores in the state, exceeding mandated goals for any state nationwide."
  - ▶ **Better:** "We have 71% member satisfaction (double that of the next highest-scoring plan, per the 2015

---

* *Usually.* Sometimes, people do fall for the smoke and sizzle. All you can do is put out the best proposal describing the success you can create, backed up by the successes you've already created.

State survey), exceeding mandated goals for any state nationwide."

Numbers aren't always available, but beg or lean on whoever necessary in your organization to get them. And whenever you have them, use them.

Show Off Client Successes

Examples of your successes with other clients are also excellent for building your case for your solution. When you provide an example, it affects the reviewers' perception of what you're explaining.

First, examples enable the reviewers to envision themselves as your client. As they read your story, they'll picture their organization, their staff, and their problem in place of the one you've described (and if you've done your research, you've made this easy for them by providing a success involving a client in circumstances similar to the issuer). By doing this, you've gotten them thinking in terms of being your client instead of just evaluating and asking whether they want to buy from you. Using our auto brochure example, the success story takes the readers from looking at the car to seeing themselves behind the wheel.

Second, examples personalize your successes. What most people want to read about is other people, so use success stories to make your proposal not just about capabilities, features, and numbers, but also the people who benefitted from working with you and how your success with them led to your outstanding statistics. And remember when we were discussing graphics and photos? Customer success stories are a prime place to use them—smiling faces not only make the reader feel more positively (even unconsciously) but will also associate the successes you're describing with happy people (again, even unconsciously).

Third, by personalizing the success with a story, it becomes tangible to the reader. For example, for all the stats and details you can throw at them about your Medicaid offering's preemie-care program, telling the story of how your doctors and nurses cared for a baby born three months early while your field reps coordinated support for the young single mother through community programs makes your program *real* in an emotional way that lists of services and statistics can't. Include a few quotes from the caregivers on their concern, some grateful words from the mom, and a smiling photo of her and her now-two-year-old, and you have more than a program description—you have an engaging and compelling story that concretely and memorably demonstrates the positive results your program creates.

Always get a signed release! Any time you quote someone or use a person's photo in your proposal, be sure to get that person to sign a photo/quote release before you publish or submit your response. Without one, you can open your organization up to all sorts of financial and legal risk from subjects who come back and claim they never gave you permission to use their image or words in your proposal.

Stick to the Style Guide

Not a lot to say here: As you're writing your answers, keep to your style guide's rules and recommendations for grammar, punctuation, layout, etc. As we discussed, doing this keeps your answers consistent and your proposal more professional for it.

Camouflage Your Weaknesses

Everybody wants to know, but nobody wants to ask:

"What if a question is about a weakness of ours?"

As you've gathered from what you've read so far, I'm big on direct responses that answer a question plainly so the reviewer can understand it immediately, score it, and move on to the next one. Which is great if the answer is highlighting one of your solution's strengths.

If a question exposes a weakness, you still need to answer it honestly—lying on a proposal is a really, *really* bad idea. You have to tell the truth.

But you don't have to make it obvious.

I call this camouflaging the answer. So far, I've talked about making answers as apparent as possible, so they leap off the page and the reader doesn't have to dig for them.

This is the one circumstance where I recommend you make the reader dig.

How you do it depends on the question. If you had a question asking for the last three years of customer satisfaction ratings you've received and you can report increasing numbers, you'd highlight them in a table or graph:

	Two Years Ago	Last Year	YTD
Customer Satisfaction Results	81%	86%	89%

or

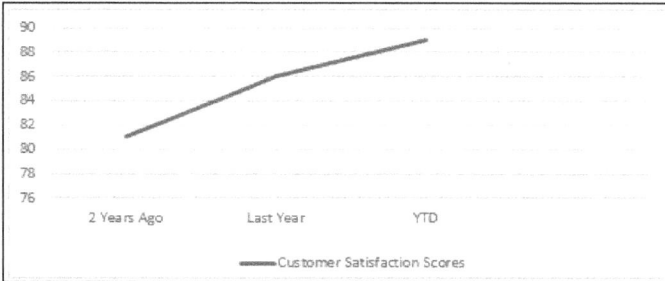

But if last year you implemented a new support policy your customers hated that caused your numbers to drop, and your replacement policy hasn't been in effect long enough to shift your satisfaction numbers upward again, a table or graph makes it obvious that your customers have taken a recent dislike to you.

	Two Years Ago	Last Year	YTD
Customer Satisfaction Results	81%	86%	53%

or

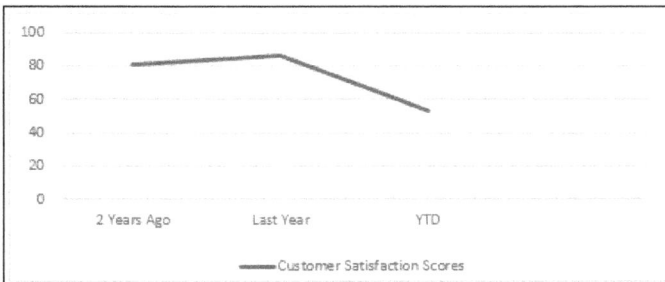

In this situation, some would opt for presenting the table or graph and adding a few lines of explanation for the dip, with a description of what efforts you're making to fix it.

But you don't want to show them that decline, so lose the graphic (by making the drop so plain, in either table or graph format it's hurting, not helping). And an explanation runs the risk of reading like you're making excuses.

Instead, get the numbers into the middle of a paragraph that explains your commitment to customer satisfaction—

—someplace where they don't stand out:

4.b. Please provide your customer satisfaction scores for two years ago, last year, and the current year-to-date.|

WTWP Enterprises is committed to the highest standards for customer satisfaction. We ensure every customer's interaction with us is resolved suitably and fairly, whether face-to-face, online, or through our customer service phone center. As a longtime partner with your organization, we understand well the needs of your membership, and what works and doesn't work in your market. With a YTD score of 53%, a two-year ago score of 81%, and a last-year score of 86%, we've been able to determine support strategies that resonate, and have effected policy changes that should push satisfaction scores up at least 5% in our next review cycle.

You haven't lied and you haven't evaded. And you didn't make it obvious that your most recent results show a clear decline. In fact, notice how by listing the poor score first that—even clearly labeled—at a glance, a reader might get the impression it's a low beginning score that's risen with each subsequent year.

A different problem might require a different solution. For example, suppose a question asks you to explain three particular functions of your vendor website but your IT group has only ever implemented two out of those three requested functions. You're looking at an answer that, if you list and explain the two you do have, at *best* can score only two-thirds of the full point value. A solution in this case might be to include with the proposal's attachments a copy of your website's vendor user manual and simply answer the question like this:

> *"The full functionality of our vendor site is explained in detail our Vendor User Manual, included as Attachment D."*

I admit, that's a gamble—you could tick off the reviewer by giving nothing and making him or her flip to another section and then page through your vendor manual. But if you have a great vendor manual, it may impress the reviewer enough that the missing feature goes unnoticed and you get a good score.

If you can't avoid showing a weakness, camouflage it so it isn't obvious and hope for the best.

Write in the Present Tense

It's an old technical writing rule to always write in the present tense—that is, tell what something *does*, not what it *will do*. Present tense makes for less wordy, more direct sentences that are easier to understand. For example:

- **Future tense:** "We will complete installation within 90 days."

  ▶ **Present tense:** "We complete installation within 90 days."

- **Future tense:** "We will reduce expenses by at least 20%."

  ▶ **Present tense:** "We reduce expenses by at least 20%."

See how the statements made in the present tense feel more concrete and factual? Future tense is a prediction of something that's going to happen (and anyone who's watched the nightly weather forecast or had a contractor do work on their house knows how predictions can go). Present tense states what *is*, and creates a sense of certainty in the reader's mind. It sounds like established fact, not something vaguely in the future—and thus uncertain.

Write in the present tense to change the perceptions of your readers and reviewers so they feel your proposal isn't just promises and predictions, but established facts.

Write in Active Voice

Back in high school, your English teacher most likely discouraged or outright banned you and your classmates from writing in the passive voice.

Just as a refresher: In active voice, the subject of the sentence performs the action, as in "The dog bit the stranger." In passive voice, the subject of the sentence has the action done to it, as in "The stranger was bitten by the dog."

Active voice is usually preferable because it's more direct and uses fewer words. It states things clearly and makes the sentence easier to read and comprehend.

Unlike your English teacher (and more than a few writing coaches and books I've encountered), I *do* think passive voice has its place in communication when it comes to the focus of a sentence—in the dog bite example in the callout, notice how one sentence is about the dog and the other is about the stranger. Even though they both describe the same event, they're different for who they're about.

At the same time, don't use focus as your excuse for bad writing—sure, "Our customers are helped by our support team." focuses on the customers, but you could keep the focus *and* make it active by saying "Our customers receive help from our support team."

Even worse, passive voice can obscure who performs an action or is responsible for it—which is the reason so many businesses and politicians like using it. Saying "Funds are transferred on the first of every month." may seem like a reasonable statement to some, but for me (or anyone trying to get a clear image of the process), it only brings up the questions *Who will transfer the funds?* and *How do they transfer them?* The passive voice, then, allows a writer to skip details the reader may really want to know.

Granted, because it uses more words and more complicated sentence structure, passive voice sounds more formal and more intellectual to some people. Although that might be helpful, remember the number-one purpose of the proposal is to answer questions in order to win business. Anything that slows the reader or obscures the facts the reader is looking for hurts your chances of getting everything across.

Include details and present information completely and directly so your readers immediately understand it.

Convey Passion

Whenever you can, work to convey passion and determination in your answers.

More than numbers, more than facts, think through what gets the people in your organization out of bed and into the office every day. Listen to the words your field reps use and note the stories your customer support managers tell. Then use that language and those stories in your response to explain why your organization does what it does and why it makes a difference for you and your clients.

Show your readers how much the people who make up your organization care and how meaningful the work is to them, and they'll see exactly why you're the top pick for the job.

Use Contractions

Some of you are flipping out again, I know, because you've been told since sixth grade that contractions have no place in formal writing. Some of you may have even be remembering unhappily when a stray *it's* or *don't* once cost you a letter grade on a term paper.

The proposal is important and formal in terms of being the starting point of a contract. But remember, as I told you, it's a conversation.

Have you ever had a conversation with someone who didn't use contractions? It sounds strange and more than a bit distant or reserved. Usually, the only people you hear speak without using contractions are characters in historical movies, aliens and robots in old sci-fi, and Grover from *Sesame Street*. All of them might be interesting to talk to, but would you buy from them?

You're trying to engage your reader with your proposal, not sound like *Star Trek's* android, Mr. Data. Avoiding contractions actually puts up a barrier between you and your readers, a big wall of formality that keeps them from connecting with you in your conversation. That's why aliens and robots are so frequently portrayed speaking this way—it makes them seem distant and inhuman. It would seem strange if someone met with you or presented to you and never used a contraction as he or she talked.

Even if you didn't pick up on it in the meeting, it would leave you feeling odd, and would probably hit you later *why* that person seemed off. And even worse for that person, while listening to that presentation, you devoted a lot of mental effort to figuring out what it was that seemed wrong about the presentation, rather than focusing on the point of it.

You want your proposal to be engaging and make your readers feel comfortable with you. Be conversational, and use contractions as you would when speaking. Then your reader can focus on what you're saying without being distracted by how you're saying it.

Use Personal Pronouns

One way you can get reviewers on your side is by becoming personal to them. That doesn't mean including baby pictures of your kids in the proposal…but it kinda does…

Often, people writing business materials like proposals refer to their organization exclusively by name, occasionally using the pronoun "it" when the name would otherwise be repeated too many times:

- "WTWP Enterprises offers its clients a unique and satisfying experience. WTWP stands behind every project, with client satisfaction WTWP's first priority."

Not terrible, but distant, and the company is clearly a thing. Now, try it this way:

- "WTWP Enterprises offers our clients a unique and satisfying experience. We stand behind every project, with client satisfaction as our first priority."

See the difference? In the second example, instead of the organization being a thing, it's become a group of people. The reader, without realizing it, has been guided into thinking in terms of the people behind the proposal instead of a faceless corporate entity.

Some of you are already thinking, "But I've always heard you should repeat the company name as often as possible, to make it stick in the reader's mind." That is true—to a point. But if you overdo it...

Remember back when Bob Dole was running for president? Remember how he had that habit of talking about himself in the third person? (*"You want to know what Bob Dole thinks about the economy? Well, Bob Dole's gonna tell you what Bob Dole thinks of the economy, right now!"*) That wasn't just an odd affectation on Senator Dole's part. Earlier in his political career, he'd been advised to repeat his name as much as possible so people would remember it. And thanks to comedian Norm McDonald's merciless impression of him on *Saturday Night Live*, every week during the campaign, it's what many people *only* remember him for.

It sounds strange to repeat a name so much. Find a balance in how often you repeat your organization name, and don't Bob Dole your proposal.

Keep Your Answer Concise

Shorter answers are easier to read and score.

Through their college and university studies, many individuals come to the conclusion (mistakenly) that longwinded, ponderous sentences, featuring both numerous clauses (and abundant parenthetical phrases) as well as obscure and lengthy polysyllabic words and/or unnecessary conjunctions, somehow elevate the perceived intellectual level and discursive underpinnings of themselves and their discourse in order to lend authority and credibility to their declarations and pronouncements—an errant assumption about prose on the parts of those individuals that leads only to nearly incomprehensible discourse that is overly formal while simultaneously repetitious and redundant and that disregards and ignores the nearly-universally understood basics of straight-forward communications, which through such consensus indicate, in fact, that the opposite is true.

See what I did there?

State things directly. A lot of consultants you'll meet out there believe, when it comes to writing, that quantity wins and the longer the answers and the bigger and more loaded with details a proposal is, the better.

Don't buy that. Keep your writing brief. Keep it direct. Keep it lean. If you can say it in four words instead of ten, say it in four. Try to impress readers with how simple and direct you are with them and "boil down" your answer to only what was asked.

It's Better Writing

The point of writing is communication. In your writing, you want to keep your readers focused on the message you're trying to get across. Get to the point of what you're telling them, and don't drag things out. By using direct statements, expressed in ordinary words in the expected order, readers readily follow what you're saying.

> "A sentence should contain no unnecessary words, a paragraph no unnecessary sentences, for the same reason that a drawing should have no unnecessary lines and a machine no unnecessary parts."
> — William Strunk, The Elements of Style

It's Easier on Your Reviewers

On the other hand, complicated writing makes it hard for readers to figure out what you're trying to tell them. Extraneous details, intricate sentences, and dense paragraphs get in the way of the message. They shift readers' focus to making sense of the words and sentences over the message they're meant to express.

Think of your proposal as a path that leads your readers to the conclusion that your solution is the best choice. Which path do you think they'll follow better: a straight, paved path that takes them by the things they asked you to show them, or a long, winding path that takes them past places they have no interest in and is so overgrown in parts that they not only may not see what you wanted them to see, but that they need a machete to hack their way through?

And Your Reviewers Will Trust You More

Have you ever asked your kid a question about something that happened and gotten a long, long, *long* answer that starts days before the incident and involves ten other people and three other locations before arriving at what you were asking about? Have you ever watched a politician get asked a question, thank the person who asked, acknowledge the importance of the question's issue, and then launch into a five-minute discourse that has nothing to do with the question?

In either case, did you hear an answer to the question asked? One you *trusted?*

Readers in general—and reviewers in particular—can sense a snow job. In fact, in sales materials (which your proposal is, remember) they're *expecting* to be misled. Anything you do to trigger that alarm, such as sentences they can't follow or paragraphs in which they can't find the point, make them suspicious of your answers and lead them to score your answers lower (or at the very least, question your competence—also not good). The first time a reviewer feels your answer is suspicious, it sets the tone for how that reviewer now approaches *all* your answers.

Suspicious reviewers don't give high scores.

Even worse, some reviewers may even extrapolate poorly-written answers as an indication of how your organization does business. If your answers seem indirect, they may view you as an organization that will be evasive when they have concerns. And if your proposal is wordy and twice as long as some of your competitors', they may question your ability to deliver on time and within budget.

Earn their trust and keep their trust by answering their questions directly and clearly.

Keep the Reviewer's Needs in Mind

Pop Quiz: What are the first two things you need to define for any communications project? If you said anything other than "Audience and Message," go back and re-highlight the *Preparation* section.

The proposal reviewers are your primary audience. Think of their needs and how you can address them in your answers. Yes, they want clear, direct, complete answers, in which all the elements are easy to locate and in the order asked. What else do you think they want?

Consider this: Depending on how many submitters there are for the RFP, each reviewer has a stack of five or ten or more responses to read. On the low end, that could mean maybe two hundred pages to read; on the high end, with supporting documents and attachments, it could be twenty thousand pages. Or *more*.

So help that reviewer out and say no more than the question requires. This is by no mean a suggestion to leave out important information. But when you look at your writing, you'll be surprised how much really doesn't need to be there.

How does this help the reviewer?

By keeping your proposal brief and to-the-point, you're acknowledging, even indirectly, that you understand the reviewer has a lot of work to do and you're not going to waste his or her time. You're also putting yourself in a prime position to win favor with the reviewer.

Think about if you had a stack of ten proposals, each averaging a thousand pages long (for reference, in total that's ten reams of paper printed double-sided). You sigh and look for where to begin, and then in the review pile you spy one that's half the size of the others. "Well," you say to yourself, "I'll just ease myself in and start with this little one."

That first proposal to be read now has an advantage, thanks to a psychological principle called the *Primacy/Recency effect*. In short, this principle describes how people remember best the first and last items within a given sequence.

By getting a reviewer to read your proposal first, you've positioned yourself to be the best remembered of the group he or she is reviewing. Plus, by being first you get to set the bar so that all the subsequent proposals read are now going to be compared to yours.

Also, remember your reviewers are human beings—human beings who have thousands of pages to read and score and who will be working long and late hours to read them all. Keeping your response brief and direct helps you here, too. Concise answers are easier for them to read and score. If the reviewers don't have to slog through your text and dig out answers from drawn-out, wordy sentences, they'll feel happier reading your proposal. And that overall more-positive feeling can translate to better scores for your answers.

| *Happy reviewers = Higher scores*

Even better, because with fewer pages and tighter writing, they can get through your proposal more easily. Your readers will be less tired and more alert, and therefore less likely to miss parts of your answers—again, helping you score the most points you can.

Pretty decent advantages just from being concise, don't you think?

Important Elements Go to the Top and to the Left

As you write, keep in mind that people don't generally read an entire page, and the longer your answer is, the less of it they're going to read.

I'm going to pause here to let you catch your breath. Have you stopped hyperventilating? Breathing okay again? Good. Now, stay with me.

Most of us expect that our readers read our pages right-to-left and top-to-bottom (if they're reading English—

it does get different for some other languages), so that on any page, they're reading the shaded area, like this:

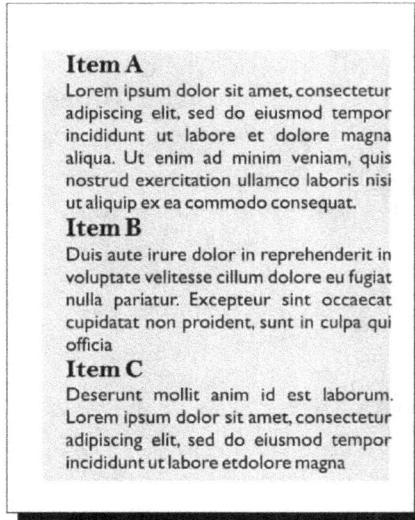

> ### Item A
> Lorem ipsum dolor sit amet, consectetur adipiscing elit, sed do eiusmod tempor incididunt ut labore et dolore magna aliqua. Ut enim ad minim veniam, quis nostrud exercitation ullamco laboris nisi ut aliquip ex ea commodo consequat.
>
> ### Item B
> Duis aute irure dolor in reprehenderit in voluptate velitesse cillum dolore eu fugiat nulla pariatur. Excepteur sint occaecat cupidatat non proident, sunt in culpa qui officia
>
> ### Item C
> Deserunt mollit anim id est laborum. Lorem ipsum dolor sit amet, consectetur adipiscing elit, sed do eiusmod tempor incididunt ut labore etdolore magna

Unfortunately for all of us writers, people don't read like this.

We can't fight or change it. But understanding this can help us lay out our answers for maximum impact on the reader.

So, if they're not reading the entire page, what *are* they reading?

Chances are, you're doing it right now, and you've been doing it since you started reading this book. Like the rest of us who are in a hurry, who have too much to read and too little time to review and process it all, they scan the page in front of them, in search of the specific point they're looking for.

Typically (again, for English-language pages and readers), they start at the top left of the page and read across. They go back to the left after each line but don't read all the way across unless what they're looking for catches their eye. This results in an area read that looks like this:

Item A
Lorem ipsum dolor sit amet, consectetur adipiscing elit, sed do eiusmod tempor incididunt ut labore et dolore magna aliqua. Ut enim ad minim veniam, quis nostrud exercitation ullamco laboris nisi ut aliquip ex ea commodo consequat.

Item B
Duis aute irure dolor in reprehenderit in voluptate velitesse cillum dolore eu fugiat nulla pariatur. Excepteur sint occaecat cupidatat non proident, sunt in culpa qui officia

Item C
Deserunt mollit anim id est laborum. Lorem ipsum dolor sit amet, consectetur adipiscing elit, sed do eiusmod tempor incididunt ut labore etdolore magna.

Or, if you have strong enough headings and sub-headings, readers may read further at the start of each section, resulting in a reading area that, because of its shape, is referred to as an F-pattern:

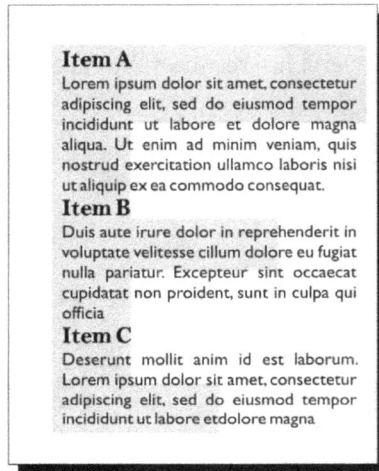

Item A

Lorem ipsum dolor sit amet, consectetur adipiscing elit, sed do eiusmod tempor incididunt ut labore et dolore magna aliqua. Ut enim ad minim veniam, quis nostrud exercitation ullamco laboris nisi ut aliquip ex ea commodo consequat.

Item B

Duis aute irure dolor in reprehenderit in voluptate velitesse cillum dolore eu fugiat nulla pariatur. Excepteur sint occaecat cupidatat non proident, sunt in culpa qui officia

Item C

Deserunt mollit anim id est laborum. Lorem ipsum dolor sit amet, consectetur adipiscing elit, sed do eiusmod tempor incididunt ut labore et dolore magna

In both patterns, you see the same basic thing: readers read most of the top and less and less as they read down the page, until they get to the bottom. Then they might read a little more than they have been, just to check for any final thing before going to the next page.

So what does ruining our illusion of an interested reader breathlessly taking in each and every carefully-selected word of our response do for us, exactly?

It tells us where to put all the important elements—the places they have the best chance of being seen.

Use the Reading Patterns for Maximum Impact

You can see from the shaded areas that readers pay the most attention to what's at the top of the page and what's on the left of the page. Put all your most important information—all your main arguments, evidence, and considerations—on those parts of the page.

The Power Spot

Your prime real estate is the first few lines at the top of the page. You can see in the diagrams, they'll read most of that. Use that area of your page to say whatever it is you want to be sure every reader sees.

Don't waste space on a background or introduction. The issuer knows their background for asking the question—they want to know what your solution is. For example, if the question asks "What will your program do to reduce expenses when implemented?" your answer definitely should *not* start with a discussion of your organization's commitment to saving money for clients—by the time you get through that, most of your readers will have shifted to reading only the first couple words of the each line.

Instead, start your answer directly:

> *"After implementation, our program reduces expenses by negotiating rate reductions with current vendors, simplifying processes, modernizing the technology used by contracted providers, and focusing on value."*

Then move on to paragraphs that explain in further detail each point you introduced.

> I'm notorious for cutting out my SMEs' introductory paragraphs. In review meetings, when we're going over each questions and response as a team, I developed a reputation for saying "I think our answer actually starts in the third paragraph…" It's not that the introductions were necessarily bad. Rather, they just took too long to get to answering the question. Often, we end up moving that intro information to someplace later in the answer, where it fleshes out or supports a particular point.

Keep to the Left

Better yet, make the paragraphs explaining each point into individual items in a bulleted list.

Reduced Expenses

After implementation, our program will reduce expenses by negotiating rate reductions with current vendors, simplifying processes, modernizing the technology used by contracted providers, and focusing on value.

- **Negotiate** rate reductions with current vendors Duis aute irure dolor in reprehenderit in voluptate velitesse
- **Simplify** processes illum dolore eu fugiat nulla pariatur.
- **Modernize** technology used by contracted providers Excepteur sint occaecat cupidatat non proident, sunt
- **Focus** on value sint occaecat cupidatat non proident, sunt in culpa qui officia

Deserunt mollit anim id est laborum.

Reduced Expenses

After implementation, our program will reduce expenses by negotiating rate reductions with current vendors, simplifying processes, modernizing the technology used by contracted providers, and focusing on value.

- **Negotiate** rate reductions with current vendors Duis aute irure dolor in reprehenderit in voluptate velitesse
- **Simplify** processes illum dolore eu fugiat nulla pariatur.
- **Modernize** technology used by contracted providers Excepteur sint occaecat cupidatat non proident, sunt
- **Focus** on value sint occaecat cupidatat non proident, sunt in culpa qui officia

Deserunt mollit anim id est laborum.

See how the list keeps the main points in the most-read area? Bullets draw the reader's eye. If next to each bullet you start with a strong, active word—preferably a verb to convey action—even a reader who's skimming the left side of the page gets an immediate sense of the solution you're proposing. The words *Reduced Expenses, Negotiate, Simplify, Modernize,* and *Focus* all leap off the page. Just a glance at your answer provides a quick outline of your solution!

The same holds true with a numbered list. If the question is asking about a process and you describe your process in the first paragraph then detail each step in a numbered list that follows, a reader needs only a quick look to get the gist of it and, hopefully, then decides to read it in detail.

Sub-Headings Reset Reader Interest

Besides breaking up long blocks of text, sub-headings also help hold reader interest by giving them something to catch their eye and interest. As you can tell in the F-pattern diagram, sub-headings essentially "re-set" the readers' tendency to read to the right less and less as they go down the page.

Item A
Item A Lorem ipsum dolor sit amet, consectetur adipiscing elit, sed do eiusmod tempor incididunt ut labore et dolore magna aliqua. Ut enim ad minim veniam, quis nostrud exercitation ullamco laboris nisi ut aliquip ex ea commodo consequat.
Item B
Duis aute irure dolor in reprehenderit in voluptate velitesse cillum dolore eu fugiat nulla pariatur. Excepteur sint occaecat cupidatat non proident, sunt in culpa qui officia
Item C
Deserunt mollit anim id est laborum. Lorem ipsum dolor sit amet, consectetur adipiscing elit, sed do eiusmod tempor incididunt ut labore et dolore magna

Item A
Item A Lorem ipsum dolor sit amet, consectetur adipiscing elit, sed do eiusmod tempor incididunt ut labore et dolore magna aliqua. Ut enim ad minim veniam, quis nostrud exercitation ullamco laboris nisi ut aliquip ex ea commodo consequat.
Item B
Duis aute irure dolor in reprehenderit in voluptate velitesse cillum dolore eu fugiat nulla pariatur. Excepteur sint occaecat cupidatat non proident, sunt in culpa qui officia
Item C
Deserunt mollit anim id est laborum. Lorem ipsum dolor sit amet, consectetur adipiscing elit, sed do eiusmod tempor incididunt ut labore et dolore magna

Use Graphics Whenever Possible

We keep coming back to this because it's that important.

As discussed in "Consider the Best Way to Answer the Question," any time you can use a graphic (chart, photo, etc.), do it. You should have already addressed whether there's an image of some kind to use when you were outlining the answer. But think about it again as you write and as you complete your answer. Is there a graph or diagram that can illustrate the information? Is there a relevant picture you can use to add visual interest?

Item A

Lorem ipsum dolor sit amet, consectetur adipiscing elit, sed do eiusmod tempor incididunt ut labore et dolore magna aliqua. Ut enim ad minim veniam, quis nostrud exercitation ullamco laboris nisi ut aliquip ex ea commodo consequat.

Item B

Duis aute irure dolor in reprehenderit in voluptate velitesse cillum dolore eu fugiat nulla pariatur. Excepteur sint occaecat cupidatat non proident, sunt in culpa qui officia

Item C

Deserunt mollit anim id est laborum.Lorem ipsum dolor sit amet, consectetur adipiscing elit, sed do eiusmod tempor incididunt ut labore et dolore magna aliqua. Ut enim ad minim

---

Item A

Lorem ipsum dolor sit amet, consectetur adipiscing elit, sed do eiusmod tempor incididunt ut labore et dolore magna aliqua. Ut enim ad minim veniam, quis nostrud exercitation ullamco laboris nisi ut aliquip ex ea commodo consequat.

Item B

Duis aute irure dolor in reprehenderit in voluptate velitesse cillum dolore eu fugiat nulla pariatur.
Excepteur sint occaecat cupidatat non proident, sunt in culpa qui officia

Item C

Deserunt mollit anim id est laborum. Lorem ipsum dolor sit amet, consectetur adipiscing elit, sed do eiusmod tempor

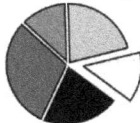

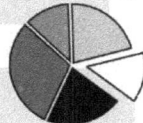

Not only does an image help set your information in the reader's mind, it can also guide your reader to look at more of the page:

Item A

Lorem ipsum dolor sit amet, consectetur adipiscing elit, sed do eiusmod tempor incididunt ut labore et dolore magna aliqua. Ut enim ad minim veniam, quis nostrud exercitation ullamco laboris nisi ut aliquip ex ea commodo consequat.

Item B

Duis aute irure dolor in reprehenderit in voluptate velitesse cillum dolore eu fugiat nulla pariatur.
Excepteur sint occaecat cupidatat non proident, sunt in culpa qui officia

Item C

Deserunt mollit anim id est laborum. Lorem ipsum dolor sit amet, consectetur adipiscing elit, sed do eiusmod tempor

---

Item A

Lorem ipsum dolor sit amet, consectetur adipiscing elit, sed do eiusmod tempor incididunt ut labore et dolore magna aliqua. Ut enim ad minim veniam, quis nostrud exercitation ullamco laboris nisi ut aliquip ex ea commodo consequat.

Item B

Duis aute irure dolor in reprehenderit in voluptate velitesse cillum dolore eu fugiat nulla pariatur.
Excepteur sint occaecat cupidatat non proident, sunt in culpa qui officia

Item C

Deserunt mollit anim id est laborum. Lorem ipsum dolor sit amet, consectetur adipiscing elit, sed do eiusmod tempor

As something different among the text, the image on the page draws the eye to it and to the text around it, where a word or phrase catches the readers' interest. Now those readers have read more of your answer than they otherwise would have, and more than the same answers from your competitors who elected not use a graphic.

Answer the Question in One Place

I had a professor in college who once explained to us why he preferred we use footnotes rather than endnotes in the papers we turned in to him: "It's just that, when I'm reading your paper and want to take a look at a citation, it's easier if I can glance at a footnote at the bottom of the page," he began. "With an endnote, it's hard for me to use a finger on one hand to hold my place, and then with my other hand flip to the back and search out your citation and smoke and drink all at the same time."

I have it on good authority most proposal reviewers feel the same way.

When you reach Question 63 and realize that you already answered that question in part C of Question 42, you may be tempted to simply answer "For this information, please see our response to Question 42, part C." Now your reviewers have to hold their place, flip back and find the answer you referred them to, read it, and then decide if it is indeed the same as the answer to Question 63. Which some will find irritating, particularly if they have several more proposals they're trying get through, not to mention if they're smoking and drinking at the same time.

Instead of directing them back to the other question, *you* do the work and put the answer from 42 right there. If it's truly the *exact* same answer, copy and paste it. However, I'm willing to bet it's different enough that it could stand a re-write to truly and match what Question 63 is asking for—remember what we discussed about canned answers and re-writing to the question before you right now?

Put the answer in front of your readers. Don't make them search for it.

Follow the 1/3 Rule for Layouts

This advice really only applies if you're the one laying out the proposal as well as writing it. However, when you're writing an answer, try to keep in mind what you need, ideally, to create a balanced page.

The 1/3 Rule is simple. It states that a well-balanced page is made up of:

- 1/3 text
- 1/3 graphics
- 1/3 empty space (also called *negative space*)

This isn't a hard and fast rule, and by no means is it precise—whatever you do, don't take a ruler to the page to measure and calculate the total area each for text, graphics, and empty space (engineers, I'm looking at you). Rather, it's a guideline to help you understand what a balanced, eye-friendly page that readers find appealing looks like.

Dense, text-heavy documents can intimidate readers. By that, I mean they can give them pause when they're reading. If a reviewer turns a page, sighs "oh, boy…" and decides to take a break right then, your narrative has lost momentum. Not only that, but how positive do you think that reader is feeling about your proposal, your solution, and your organization at that point? Part of the objective when laying out a page, then, is to balance text, graphics, and white space to make the page easier to read and *inviting* to your reader.

> *"Ideal" is the key word in the 1/3 Rule—realistically, you won't have a relevant graphic for every page, and overused callouts can become cluttering. Strive for the ideal, but work with what you have and at least maintain a good balance of positive space and negative space (content space and empty space) on each page.*

On the following pages are examples of the first pages from two well-known books. Which one is friendlier to your eye? Which one draws you into its story? Which one gets all its information across with the least work for the reader?

CHAPTER I
LOOMINGS

CALL me Ishmael. Some years ago—never mind how long precisely—having little or no money in my purse, and nothing particular to interest me on shore, I thought I would sail about a little and see the watery part of the world. It is a way I have of driving off the spleen and regulating the circulation. Whenever I find myself growing grim about the mouth; whenever it is a damp, drizzly November in my soul; whenever I find myself involuntarily pausing before coffin warehouses, and bringing up the rear of every funeral I meet; and especially whenever my hypos get such an upper hand of me, that it requires a strong moral principle to prevent me from deliberately stepping into the street, and methodically knocking people's hats off—then, I account it high time to get to sea as soon as I can. This is my substitute for pistol and ball. With a philosophical flourish Cato throws himself upon his sword; I quietly take to the ship. There is nothing surprising in this. If they but knew it, almost all men in their degree, some time or other, cherish very nearly the same feelings toward the ocean with me.

There now is your insular city of the Manhattoes, belted round by wharves as Indian isles by coral reefs—commerce surrounds it with her surf. Right and left, the streets take you waterward. Its extreme down-town is the battery, where that noble mole is washed by waves, and cooled by breezes, which a few hours previous were out of sight of land. Look at the crowds of water-gazers there.

Circumambulate the city of a dreamy Sabbath afternoon. Go from Corlears Hook to Coenties Slip, and from thence, by Whitehall, northward. What do you see?—Posted like silent sentinels all around the town, stand thousands upon thousands of mortal men fixed in ocean reveries. Some leaning against the spiles; some seated upon the pier-heads; some looking over the bulwarks of ships from China; some high aloft in the rigging, as if striving to get a still better seaward peep. But these are all landsmen; of week days pent up in lath and plaster—tied to counters, nailed to benches, clinched to desks. How then is this? Are the green fields gone? What do they here?

But look! here come more crowds, pacing straight for the water, and seemingly bound for a dive. Strange! Nothing will content them but the extremest limit of the land; loitering under the shady lee of yonder warehouses will not suffice. No. They must get just as nigh the water as they possibly can without falling in. And there they stand—miles of them—leagues. Inlanders all, they come from lanes and alleys,

The sun did not shine.
It was too wet to play.
So we sat in the house
All that cold, cold, wet day.

Now, most importantly, which page did you *read?*

A Few Tips on Microsoft Word

If you're like the 80% of people out there who use Microsoft Word at work, indulge me for a minute and let me share two important tips:

- **Always use Word's style functions to format your proposal.** Formatting by hand, even with Word's Format Painter, is bad! Using styles not only makes revising the format of your document at any time almost instantaneous, it also enables you to use many of the automatic functions in Word.

- **Use Word's automatic functions whenever you can.** Please say this with me:

"Word is not a typewriter."

I've stared aghast at the things I've seen people try to do in Word with the space bar and paragraph returns. Word has powerful functions that can automatically generate a table of contents or index, number and lay out captions and footnotes, and link and maintain cross-references within your document—all of which can be updated instantly by pressing the F9 key. If you're flipping through your file and trying to do any of these tasks by hand, you're needlessly losing hours and hours of time you could spend polishing your proposal!

This is a subject worthy of a book of its own, so right now I'll just urge you to spend some time learning how Word works, and start taking advantage of what it can do for you. Once you understand its features, you'll wonder how you got anything done before, when you were doing captions and footnotes and tables of contents by hand.

Attachments

Something else, more for the members of your team who are laying out your document than for those doing the writing: Attachments. Does the RFP require you to submit a copy of your organization's license to do business in the issuer's state? Copies of specific certifications? A list of the partners who make up your network nationally?

Although I'm typically in favor of keeping things right on the page where they're mentioned, copies of agreements, lists, and reports can have dozens or even hundreds of pages, and inserts of more than a single page can really break the flow of your proposal. Lengthy inserts, then, can make your proposal seem disjointed. They can clutter your responses and scatter your answers, costing you both focus and momentum in your narrative.

Instead, place those materials at the back of your proposal as attachments. With each attached document individually numbered and labeled, a well-arranged attachments section can house them all in one place where each one can be easily located.

Whenever you do this, back in your answer to the question, be sure to point the reader to the *specific* place where the attachment is. Sounds obvious, maybe, but I've seen proposals where the writers directed the reviewers to the attachments with the phrase "That information has been included hereto as an attachment."

What?

Aside from the use of "hereto" (we're in a conversation, remember, and when was the last time you heard anyone say "hereto"?) as a reader, my first question is, "Where's the attachment?" And my second question is, "Now I have to dig all through the end of this thing and figure out which attached list is the one I need to see for this answer?"

Remember what we discussed about keeping your reviewer happy?

Be sure to label all your attachments. And when you refer to them, if for some reason you can't note a specific page number in the reference, at least give an attachment number to all your attachments and call out each that way. Then in your answer, direct readers to it with a phrase like, "For the complete list, see Attachment D."

Organize your proposal. Do the extra work and make things easy for your reviewers to find. It'll pay off in your score.

Editing

When your answers are written and done, if you're lucky, your organization is springing for a professional editor to edit and proofread your proposal. If you're like the rest of us, though, it's time to start editing.

> *Although proofreading is part of editing, editing and proofreading aren't the same thing! Editing is an overall review of the text to make sure it's clear, organized effectively, and makes sense. Proofreading, on the other hand, focuses on finding typos and dropped punctuation and identifying and correcting errors in spelling, grammar, and formatting. Because editing involves re-writing and reorganizing, it needs to be completed before proofreading begins.*

For a proposal, there are six steps to the final edit:

1. Review your completed response.

2. Review any Q&A documents, amendments, or other revisions issued for the RFP.

3. Change your response appropriately, based on the state's updates.

4. Get fresh eyes on your completed response.

5. Hold a Red Team Review.

6. Proofread the response for errors.

Review Your Completed Response

If you're a SME, "your response" means the answers you wrote to the questions you were assigned. If you're one of the dedicated members of the Proposal Management Team (proposal manager, writer, sales/marketing, executive), it means the entire proposal.

Either way, the process is the same: read a question, then read the answer and ask:

• *Does the response answer the question directly and clearly?*

When you read the answer, you should immediately be able to identify each item the question asked about and understand how your answer addresses it. If any part of the question isn't addressed or if any part of the answer doesn't make sense as you read it, you need to re-write.

- *Does the response incorporate the Win theme?*

When you read the answer, can you identify how it ties to the Win Theme that was defined for the proposal? Again, depending on your Win Theme and the specific question, it may not make sense for the question to address the Win Theme—for a question asking you to list your organization's business licenses in a state, a Win Theme involving the cost savings your organization can provide probably doesn't figure into the answer; however, a Win Theme portraying you as a long-term partner *would* apply, since you could bring up how long you've held those licenses while working with the proposal issuer.

- *Does everything in your response belong there?*

If the question doesn't ask for it, take it out of your answer! You want your answers to be lean and direct so they're immediately understood. If a reader would question why you added a specific piece of information, either re-write to make the connection more clear or cut it. You don't want your reviewer to stop and try to figure out a connection between their question and your answer. And as I mentioned before, you *never* want reviewers to realize they're not even sure what question you're answering.

- *Get rid of the fluff—if it's not directly answering the question, cut it out!*

Usually, proposal fluff falls into two categories: introductions and unnecessary words and phrases.

▶ **Introductions,** as we've already discussed, are usually overviews and explanations your readers don't need. Again, if the issuer wants to know how your health program will address childhood obesity, three paragraphs at the beginning of your answer explaining the importance of addressing childhood obesity not only wastes the readers' time (if they didn't think it's important, they wouldn't have devoted a question to it) but also costs you their attention (both by boring them with something they already know and by squandering the power spot at the top of the page, where you still have their full attention).

▶ **Unnecessary words and phrases** are where you really get to put on the editor hat (or visor, if you watch really old movies). These are words or strings of words people use to pad out their writing so they look like they've written more or to sound more intelligent or well-spoken. For example

– Why say "We accept late, delayed, and overdue payments" when "We accept late payments" says the same thing in fewer words? All the extra words do is make the sentence longer and show you have access to a thesaurus.

– In the next political debate you watch, count how many times the politicians start a response with phrases like "In the very near future" or "In the event that" or "At this current point in time". This is a public speaking trick used to stall while formulating an answer. Because people have grown used to hearing these unnecessary stalling phrases, they've crept into writing. Instead, be direct. You can get the same ideas across as those phrases by simply saying "Soon" or "If" or "Now".

- Extra words aren't always extra descriptive. "Very professional staff", "future outlook", and "past history" are all expressions I've seen in proposals. But they say no more than just "professional staff", "outlook", and "history" do—and they say it in half as many words.

Cut the unnecessary words and keep your writing lean, clean, and direct.

Review Any Amendments

Issuers can—and do—issue RFP revisions that ask for information not requested in the initial RFP. These can be revisions to existing questions that come out of the clarifying questions you and the other bidders submit, or sometimes they're items the issuer either forgot to include in the initial RFP or just now realized they need.

Either way, you have to evaluate the amendments and then scope out their effect on your proposal—on the answers you've already written, on the supporting materials you've attached, or the new answers they require you to write. The good thing is: you've gone through the process once already, so this pass to incorporate the amended materials gives you a chance to focus your answer further.

This is not a step to skip. Always make sure *everything* the issuer has asked for is included in your response!

Revise Based on the Amendments

You've already been through the initial proposal, and you've evaluated the amendments so you know what material you need to revise, and what new material you need to add.

Once you've identified how the RFP amendments affect the current draft of your proposal, do one thing before you start making changes: Save your current version under a new name. Whether you name it "First Draft" or "Old Proposal" or "v01", take the draft you have right now and stash a copy of it on your network, your hard drive, on a flash drive, *wherever*. But trust me, as you're working on the revisions, at some point you're going to be in the middle of changing an answer and realize there's some piece of the answer that covered something better than how you have it currently in the revision, and you'll want to look at the previous version for reference,

With that copy of your first draft saved someplace safe, you can begin revising any old answers and writing the new answers the amendments require. This is the same process you followed before, so you should be feeling like a pro by now.

Get Fresh Eyes

As a last step in your edit, get someone else to read over your proposal. At this point, you've been working pretty closely on it for some time, and you have a tendency now to see things as you expect them to be, not as they are. Someone who hasn't read your document yet doesn't bring those same preconceptions when reading it, and can therefore see some of the errors and patches of rough writing you've missed.

> *Who's a good candidate to be your fresh eyes? Anyone you can find—a teammate, your manager, one of the other SMEs on the proposal, your spouse, or your college-age kid who's home for the summer. Look for someone you can beg a few hours from to read over the response you wrote and give you feedback.*

Once your fresh eyes reader has looked over your response, ask him or her some simple questions:

- *Could you find the response to each point the RFP question asked?*

  ► If the fresh eyes reader couldn't find all the points from the question immediately, you need to re-write to make them stand out and easily identifiable.

- *Could you follow the answer to the question?*

  ► If your response lost your fresh eyes reader, you need to re-write.

- *Did you understand why each part of the answer was there?*

  ► If your fresh eyes reader doesn't see the reason some portion of your answer belongs in the answer, consider cutting it out.

Once you've completed this editing step, the best thing you can do (if there's time—there *is* a deadline looming) is repeat it. Writing is an iterative process, and each round of feedback and each resulting re-write helps you both round out and focus your answers.

Hold a Red Team Review

This is a step more for big proposals with longer deadlines (usually government contracts) than it is for smaller proposals. If you're a solo proposal manager putting out several RFP responses per month, this is most likely something you flat don't have time for (but don't skip this section and read ahead—you may find an idea or principle you want to use).

Red Team reviews began in the military as a method to have a knowledgeable, critical group assess plans and strategies. It's common today for proposals (especially large government proposals), and really, it serves the same purpose here as in the military—to evaluate effectiveness.

This process can take a very long time, a full day or several days, depending on the size of the proposal. Schedule and get commitments accordingly.

Who's on the Red Team?

Who should attend the Red Team meeting? Your full Proposal Management Team, first and foremost (that includes your "Secret Weapon" SMEs). They're the ones most familiar with the RFP at this point, and they understand what it's asking for as well as your Win Themes and writing approach (such as the conversational tone, using contractions and personalized pronouns, etc.). Additionally, if they haven't been involved already, bring in representatives from your Legal department, field reps (sales, network, etc.), and executive management (if it's a big prospect, they'll probably want to be there).

What Happens in Red Team?

For me, Red Team is a bit like the Table Reading we did at the beginning, where everybody—the Proposal Management Team and additional players—get together in one room and close the door. What's worked best for me is to use a projector to shine the proposal on the wall and, starting at page 1, read through the entire thing as a group, page by page, with everyone commenting where they think something needs work.

Together, you all decide if each question's response:

- Answers the question
- Makes sense
- Is correct
- Is complete, with nothing extraneous (i.e., the question covers what it needs to and everything in the answer belongs there)
- Is presented well (text, graphics, design, and layout all making for an attractive, eye-friendly page)

Revise right then and there as needed.

Proofread the Response for Errors

Once everything is re-written and done the way you want, proofread the proposal for errors. There are entire books on proofreading, so I won't even attempt to summarize the process. But remember, proofreading is about finding typos, punctuation errors, and formatting and style inconsistencies, to make the final document as clean and error-free as possible.

Note that I said "as error-free as possible." With an RFP's typically short timeframe and strict deadline, you're going to have errors, whether a typo, missing period, or extra space. Make sure your numbers and what you're committing to are all 100% correct, and don't sweat it if after submission you discover you used "to" instead of "too" once, missed the "e" at the end of a word, or dropped an Oxford comma someplace.

Chapter 4: The Executive Summary

I have one last Secret of Writing I'll let you in on:

Some decision-makers will *never* read your proposal.

I know, I know…You've put so much time and expense into writing it: researching the issuer's needs, figuring out what the evaluators are looking for, and tailoring your answers to it all. "How can anyone decide about our proposal without reading it?" you ask.

Trust me, they will. Rather than read your full proposal, those decision-makers rely on two things:

- Their reviewers' evaluations of your proposal
- Your proposal's executive summary

Yes, to make their decisions, some readers will rely on just a few sheets at the front of a package that is hundreds or even thousands of pages thick. So, in addition to winning answers, at the beginning you need a killer summary.

Summarize

To win over those decision-makers, you need a great executive summary that says everything your proposal says about your organization and your solution—in only a tiny fraction of the space. This is why, even though it's at the front of your proposal, I recommend writing the executive summary toward the end of the project, when the proposal is mostly done (your proposal has to present things in the order asked—that doesn't mean you have to write it all in the order asked). By the end, you've been answering questions and fine-tuning your message for a while and have a good idea of what your proposal is about, so you'll have a solid grasp of what it is you're trying to summarize.

Traditionally, the executive summary is considered an introduction to and overview of your proposal, a few paragraphs up to a few pages that tell who you are and highlight all the important elements of the proposal. Today, however, most proposal advice emphasizes the executive summary as a sales pitch, where you outline all the main selling points of your proposed solution.

If you've been writing your proposal answers as I've recommended, guess what? All along, you've been identifying your strengths not as features, but as solutions to the issuer's problem. And you've been tying them to your Win Theme. So if you go back and highlight the relevant points you've written so far, you have an outline for your executive summary. That, with a little fleshing out, will give you a good summary.

Now, if you want to write a *great* summary, keep reading.

More Than Facts: Tell a Story

I'm a storyteller by trade and I know that if there's one thing almost everyone loves, that almost everyone will stop and pay attention to, it's a good story. And I'm not just talking about the latest kid wizard or teen vampire books, Netflix binge, or telenovela.

Storytelling is the best way to engage an audience, which is why it figures into nearly everything you see on TV—even the stuff that's supposed to be nonfiction.

It's only the veneer of reality that makes most TV reality series *seem* immediate. What keeps them compelling (and the audiences coming back week after week) is the storytelling. Were you aware that not just news but almost all "reality" shows have a full staff of writers? They don't make up the story, but their job is to watch the video shot on that island or backstage with all the talent contestants and figure out how to create a compelling narrative. They make that castaway on that beach seem a despicable villain and that fifteen-year-old ingénue a teary-eyed underdog you'll root for to out-talent the rest of the contestants.

You can even see it in your favorite news magazine shows. They *could* tell you in just a couple sentences about the doctor who faked her death and started over in a new city. Instead, they tease it out over an hour, reenacting arguments in her marriage, detailing her husband's grief at her apparent death and his suspicions about the seemingly failed brakes he'd just had replaced. And then in the last ten minutes of the show: the stunning revelation portraying how he discovered the truth when he happened across a news story about an elderly park-goer who was struck by an errant frisbee and saved by a quick-thinking hot dog vendor who turned out to be his presumed-dead physician wife.

It's all a story.

So tell your readers a story. Find a way that your interaction with a current customer improved things for that customer. Show how your latest machine controller kept a century-old, family-owned metal forming business from going under. Or how your communications service saved a life. Or how your medical supply delivery eased the pain of an elderly emphysema patient. Get the reader involved, and show how your solution changes the lives of businesses and people for the better.

Draw them into your story, and like getting read first, your proposal sets the bar that all the others have to measure up to.

Chapter 5: Go Out There and *Win!*

You really don't need me cheering you on—this is writing to gain business, not a high school cross-country meet. So you're going to do it, and you need to win (if you want to stay in business). Instead, let me offer a little advice and a bit of perspective for the writers and the non-writers who've gotten this far and read through all the methods suggested, with the goal of winning RFP business.

For the Writers

I've talked to writers who've confided uneasily that they've never written a proposal before and they're not sure if they can do it.

You know what? I never wrote a proposal until I wrote one.

"Well, *duh*," (or something close) you said to yourself reading that last statement. But think about it. If you're doing something new, learning a new skill, you have to start somewhere. And you won't do everything perfectly—or even well—when you start. You need to be okay with not hitting the target every time at first. Give yourself space to not be perfect at it right away as you learn your way around this new application of your skills.

Remember, as a writer—whether a technical writer or marketing writer or business writer—your job is to *communicate*. As I asked you to highlight at the beginning of Chapter 3, the first thing you do on any project is define your audience and message, and then define the most effective way to communicate that message to that audience. Whether software instructions, a product brochure, or a weekly internal newsletter, you're already doing that.

A proposal isn't any different.

Yes, it's going to take stretching your skills in some new directions and learning to think a little differently from what you're accustomed to. But if you've been writing successfully so far, you already have the skill set to go through an RFP and work with your Proposal Management Team and SMEs to get the questions answered.

If this is something you're interested in doing, trust me, you *can* figure it out and get it done.

For Everyone Else

For the project manager, business analyst, engineer, nurse, keep this in mind:

Your job isn't to write.

Does that make you feel better?

Your writer's job is to write. The writer will take what you give him or her and then pound it into the shape of a clear, concise, professional response. Your job is to give your writer the information needed to answer the RFP question.

That doesn't let you off the hook entirely. Anything you can do to help your writer focus on the things that need focusing on, you should do. You've read this far, so you already know about organizing your answer so it follows the order things were asked in the question. You know about writing in the present tense, echoing the question's language in your answer, and everything else in Chapter 3. Think about all those tips and apply them when you draft your answer.

Most of all, don't be intimidated. Writing the response, as I keep emphasizing, is just getting into a conversation. And even the most socially awkward engineers and software developers I've worked with on technical writing projects have had conversations (really, I've seen it). Start with bullet points to get you going. Then just write what you'd say to someone to explain whatever it is. If you have to, literally talk it through on your phone using a speech-to-text app to transcribe it for you and email it to yourself so you can rewrite what you dictated. Unlike your writer, this *is* a new skill for you. But as I said, you've had conversations before. You can do this.

In the unlikely but not-unheard-of event that you're a project manager, product manager, or anyone else whose primary job isn't communications but you've been charged with producing the proposal for an RFP response, I'll tell you the same thing: You can do this. I won't lie, it's going to be harder for you without a writer. But like I told the engineers a paragraph back, you've had conversations before. Follow the processes described throughout this book, use the tips, and you can write a proposal. A winning proposal.

Now go out there and win!

Index

References

Asner, Michael. *Bulletproof RFPs*. Washington, D.C.: International City/County Management Assoc., 2003. Print.

Bigman, Alex. "6 Principles of Visual Hierarchy for Designers." *99designs Blog*. 99designs, 14 Oct. 2016. Web. 20 April 2017.

"Baby's Smile Is a Natural High." *ScienceDaily*. ScienceDaily, 08 July 2008. Web. 17 May 2017.

Browning, Beverly A. *Perfect Phrases for Writing Grant Proposals*. Maidenhead: McGraw-Hill Professional, 2008. Print.

Cherry, Kendra. "Are You a Visual, Auditory, Reading/Writing, or Tactile Learner?" *Verywell*. Verywell, 5 June 2017. Web. 17 June 2017.

"How the Human Eye Reads a Website." *Creative Bloq*. Creative Bloq Art and Design Inspiration, 24 Nov. 2014. Web. 20 April 2017.

Griffiths, Sarah. "Your Brain Really IS Faster than You Think: It Takes just 13 Milliseconds to See an Image, Scientists Discover." *Daily Mail Online*. Associated Newspapers, 20 Jan. 2014. Web. 17 May 2017.

Hatfield, Elaine, John T. Cacioppo, and Richard L. Rapson. "Mechanisms of Emotional Contagion: I. Emotional Mimicry/synchrony." *Emotional Contagion* (n.d.): 7-47. Web. 18 May 2017.

Jacob, Céline, and Nicolas Guéguen. "The Effect of Employees' Verbal Mimicry on Tipping." *International Journal of Hospitality Management* 35 (2013): 109-11. Web. 30 June 2017

Kulesza, Wojciech, Dariusz Dolinski, Avia Huisman, and Robert Majewski. "The Echo Effect." *Journal of Language and Social Psychology* 33.2 (2013): 183-201. Web. 30 June 2017

Melville, Herman. *Moby-Dick; or, The Whale.* London: Constable & Co., 1922. Bartleby.com. Web. 28 February 2017. <http://www.bartleby.com/91>.

Normand, Vrinda. *The Online Sales Blueprint.* Felton: Irresistible Online Marketing, 2014. *Irresistible Marketing.* Irresistible Online Marketing, Inc. Web. 28 February 2017. <http://www.irresistiblemarketing.com/docs/OnlineSalesBlueprintBook.pdf>.

Office, Anne Trafton. "In the Blink of an Eye." *MIT News.* MIT, 16 Jan. 2014. Web. 17 May 2017.

"Original The Art of War Translation (Not Giles)." *Sonshi Educational Resource for Sun Tzu's The Art of War,* Sonshi Group, www.sonshi.com/original-the-art-of-war-translation-not-giles.html. Web. 23 April 2017.

Sant, Tom. *Persuasive Business Proposals: Writing to Win More Customers, Clients, and Contracts.* New York: AMACOM, 2012. Print.

Sonnby-Borgstrom, Marianne. "Automatic Mimicry Reactions as Related to Differences in Emotional Empathy." *Scandinavian Journal of Psychology* 43.5 (2002): 433-43. Web. 29 June 2017

Strunk, William. *The Elements of Style.* New York: Macmillan, 1976. Print.

Sousa, David A. *How the Brain Learns.* Thousand Oaks, CA: Corwin, a Sage, 2006. Print.

Seuss, Dr. *The Cat in the Hat.* Random House, 1957. Print.

Wroblewski, Luke. "Communicating with Visual Hierarchy." *LukeW Ideation + Design.* LukeW Ideation + Design. Web. 23 Apr. 2017. <http://static.lukew.com/pageheirarchy_lukew_03192008.pdf>.

Thanks for reading this Factual Planet Chronicle. Knowledge unshared is knowledge lost, so if you loved this book, be sure to share it with your friends and followers or post a short review with your favorite bookseller or forum!

About the Author

Patrick Dorsey, owner of Mightier Than The Sword Consulting, is a professional business writer who helps people and organizations tell their stories to create success. Author of the Knights Templar adventure novel *God's Forge* as well as the eerie collection of true firsthand accounts of neighborhood ghosts *Haunted Webster Groves*, he's now sharing his expertise from twenty-five years of leading successful technical writing and business communication projects, beginning with his insights and methods for gaining business through writing RFP responses in *Write the Winning Proposal*.

Learn more about his consulting at MightierThanTheSwordConsulting.com, visit his author homepage at PatrickDorsey.com, or follow him on Twitter @PTDorsey.

If you're interested in asking Patrick Dorsey to attend or speak at your next event, please call 314.884.0057 or email Contact@LegendaryPlanet.com.

Also by Patrick Dorsey from Factual Planet and Legendary Planet

Haunted Webster Groves

God's Forge

www.ingramcontent.com/pod-product-compliance
Lightning Source LLC
Chambersburg PA
CBHW070928270326
41927CB00011B/2772